SECOND EDITION 4

Super Practice Book

SUPER PRACTICE

Garan Holcombe

CAMBRIDGE UNIVERSITY PRESS

Map of the book

Present simple questions

Language focus

Use **simple present** questions to ask people about habits and routines.
Yes/No questions are formed with **be** or **do**:

Are *you from Izmir?*	*Yes, I am.*	*No, I'm not.*
Are *we / they from Istanbul?*	*Yes, we / they are.*	*No, we / they aren't.*
Is *he / she from Bursa?*	*Yes, he / she is.*	*No, he / she isn't.*
Do *you / we / they like playing the guitar?*	*Yes, I / we / they do.*	*No, I / we / they don't.*
Does *he / she love watching films?*	*Yes, he / she does.*	*No, he / she doesn't.*

'Wh' questions are formed by putting **where**, **what**, **why**, etc., before **be** or **do**:

What *is your favourite type of music?*

1 **Complete the questions with either *do / does* or the correct form of *be*.**

6.35 p.m.

Hi, Liam

We're doing a project in school about people's lives. I've got some questions for you. Please send me your answers soon!

a ____Do____ you do any sports?

b ____________ you often tired after school?

c What ____________ you like doing at the weekend?

d Where ____________ your mother from?

Love, Zoe

2 Match the questions from Activity 1 with the answers below.

7.05 p.m.

Hi, Zoe

Thanks for your questions! Here are my answers.

1 Yes, I am. I often feel very sleepy in the evening. [b]

2 Lots of things! I go running with my brother. I watch films. Oh, I draw too. I love drawing. [ ]

3 China. I always speak Mandarin with her. I love it! [ ]

4 Yes, I do. I swim three times a week and I play basketball on Sunday mornings. [ ]

Good luck with your project!

Love, Liam

3 Complete the dialogue with the words from the box.

does ~~what~~ don't who live Yes

Mehmet (1) What does your brother do, Nick?
Nick He's a journalist.
Mehmet Really? Is it an exciting job?
Nick I (2) ________ know. I think he likes it.
Mehmet (3) ________ does he work for?
Nick He writes for the *El País* newspaper. In Spain.
Mehmet What (4) ________ he write about?
Nick He interviews famous people – actors, singers.
Mehmet Does he (5) ________ in Madrid?
Nick (6) ________, he does. In a place called La Latina.

Past simple questions

Language focus

Use **past simple questions** to ask what people did at a specific time in the past.

Yes/No questions are formed with **was** / **were** or **did**:

Were *you at the park yesterday?*	*Yes, I was.*	*No, I wasn't.*
Was *he / she in the cinema?*	*Yes, he / she was.*	*No, he / she wasn't.*

The question form with **did** is the same for every person, i.e. **I**, **he**, **she**, **they**:

Did *you / he / she / we / they go surfing?*

'Wh' questions are formed by putting **Where**, **What**, **Why**, etc., before **was** / **were** and **did**:

Where *were you on Saturday?* ***Where*** *did you go on holiday?*

1 Complete the questions and answers about a holiday in Italy.

1. ___Were___ you happy on holiday? — Yes, we ___were___.
2. ________ your brother with you? — No, he ________. He had to work.
3. ________ you go to Venice? — No, we ________. We went to Rome.
4. ________ your parents like Italy? — Yes, they ________. They want to go back next year!
5. ________ the people friendly? — Yes, they ________. They taught me some Italian.

2 Are the questions correct or incorrect? Correct the questions you think are incorrect.

1 What do you do yesterday?

Incorrect. What did you do yesterday?

2 Were you at school yesterday?

3 Do you go to the beach last summer?

4 Was you tired this morning?

5 What was the last film you saw?

6 Do you did your homework last night?

3 Answer the questions from Activity 2.

1

2

3

4

5

6

Reading: a poem

1 **Read the poem, then put questions a–f in the correct order.**

The Questioner

Do you like your school, your house, your life?
Do you eat your food with a fork and knife?
Do you have adventures big and small?
Do you think of yesterday at all?
When you were young
What did you do?

Did you go on dodgems bright and new?
Were rollercoasters white and blue?
On roundabouts, without a care,
Did the boys and girls have golden hair?
Are you different now
You know much more?
Or are you as you were before?

The past simple is present now,
The moments come and go, and how!
We go on asking questions, yes,
But what's the last one?
Can you guess?

a When you were young, what did you do? ☐
b Are you different now? ☐
c Were rollercoasters white and blue? ☐
d Do you like your school, your house, your life? 1
e What's the last one? ☐
f Do you have adventures big and small? ☐

1 **Match the words with the definitions.**

1 rhythm
2 rhyme
3 verse
4 poet
5 poem

a This is writing with short sentences (called lines) and using words that often rhyme.
b This is someone who writes poems.
c This is when the ends of two words have the same sound, e.g. *cat / hat, blue / do, door / floor.*
d This is how the words sound together.
e This is a group of lines that forms part of a poem. 'The Questioner' has three of these.

Help with Writing

Poems are not easy to write in another language. Think of words that rhyme, e.g. *fat*, *hat*, *cat*, *mat*. Then try writing a simple poem with a simple rhythm, e.g. *My dog is fat, he wears a hat, he hates the cat, she chews his mat.*

2 **Complete the poem with the words from the box.**

~~me~~ Jo floors low

The Treasure Hunt

'Where is the gold, the gold?' said Lee.
'What gold? What gold?' said Tom to (1) me.
I did not know, so turned to go,
And talked to Sue and Mark and (2) ______.
We looked at maps, for clues and doors,
And holes in walls and wooden (3) ______.
We looked up high, we looked down (4) ______,
Until it was our time to go.

3 **Now write another verse for the poem. Follow the rhythm of the verses.**

______

______

______

Listening: adventures

1 01 **Listen and tick ✓ or cross ✗.**

Activities	Daisy 	Mike 
1 	✗	✓
2 		
3 		
4 		
5 		

2 02 **Listen to Jacob talk about his adventure. Circle the correct answers.**

1 Which mountain did Jacob climb?

(a) Cave Mountain.

b Castle Mountain.

2 How did he get to the mountain?

a By train.

b By car.

3 Who did he go with?

a His parents and his brother.

b His parents.

4 What did Jacob think of the climb?

a It was fun, but it was dangerous too.

b It was dangerous and it wasn't fun.

5 How long did Jacob walk for?

a Two hours.

b Four hours.

6 Which mountain does Jacob want to climb next?

a Diamond Mountain.

b Treasure Mountain.

1 Look and write. Then play the *You can … too* game.

What's Number 2?

Go on a big wheel. You can go on a roller coaster, too!

d**rive**____
d________ ________

g________ on a
b________ ________

r________ a b________

f________ a k________

c________ a m________

w________ on the
b________

2 Work with a friend. Talk about the things to do in Activity 1.

Do you like going on a big wheel?

No, I don't. I'm scared of it! What about you?

I love going on a big wheel. It's exciting!

3 With your friend, imagine you went on an adventure yesterday. What did you do? Think of four activities. Then talk about your adventure.

Yesterday, Tom and I went on an adventure. We went to a castle at the top of a mountain. We rode our bikes to get to the mountain, and we climbed the mountain to get to the castle. We looked for treasure in the castle and we found a statue!

1 Must / Mustn't

Language focus

Use **must** to talk about what it is necessary to do, e.g. *I **must** buy my mother a birthday card.* Use **mustn't** to tell someone not to do something, e.g. *You **mustn't** play the drums so loudly.*

We do not add an **-s** to the third person with **must**. We say *He **must** do his homework* not ~~*He musts do his homework*~~.

1 Read what Maria says, then circle the correct verbs to complete the sentences.

'Mum and Dad say I don't do enough to help them with the chores. I'm going to show them how much I can do. To help me, I've got a list of things I must and mustn't do. I'm going to put it on my wall in my room …'

1 I *must* / *mustn't* tidy my room at least once a month.
2 I *must* / *mustn't* leave my clothes on the floor.
3 I *must* / *mustn't* wash the dishes at weekends.
4 I *must* / *mustn't* help Dad in the garden on Sunday afternoons.
5 I *must* / *mustn't* help Mum wash her car once a month.
6 I *must* / *mustn't* put dirty plates on the floor.

2 Complete the story with the verbs from the box.

clean	~~wear~~	be	learn	toast	use

The Never-ending Orders of
Old King Marvin

Old King Marvin lived in a huge castle near Learnum Wood. His favourite thing was telling people what to do. 'You mustn't (1) wear your crown in the garden,' he said every morning to Good Queen Tess. 'It might fall off.'

A handsome young knight called Gordon the Magnificent lived in the castle too. 'You must (2) ________ your shield and helmet,' Old King Marvin said to Gordon. 'And you must (3) ________ how to use your sword. But you mustn't (4) ________ it inside the castle.'

One morning, Old King Marvin went to the kitchen. 'I would like to make breakfast this morning,' he said to the cook. 'Is that all right?' 'Yes, sir,' said the cook. Ten minutes later, Good Queen Tess heard a loud voice in the kitchen. 'I'm very sorry, sir, but you must (5) ________ the bread for thirty-three seconds longer. You must (6) ________ careful with bread. It's easy to get it wrong.' Good Queen Tess smiled to herself, happy to hear someone telling her husband what to do for a change.

3 Look at the pictures. Complete the sentences using *must* and *mustn't*.

The Newbury Park Rules

1 You mustn't climb the trees.

2 You ________ your rubbish in the bin.

3 You ________ on the flowers.

4 You ________ your dog on a lead.

5 You ________ in the lake.

6 You ________ the ducks.

Direct and indirect objects

Language focus

Use **direct and indirect objects** to talk about things or people affected by the action of the verb.

Subject	**Verb**	**Indirect object**	**Direct object**
Jeremy	*gave*	*David*	*the book.*
I	*made*	*my sister*	*a sandwich.*
Don't	*show*	*me*	*the answer.*

The direct object is the person or thing affected by the action of the verb. It answers the question **what**, e.g. *What did Jeremy give to David?*

The indirect object is also the person or thing affected by the action of the verb; it answers the question **who**, e.g. *Who did Jeremy give the book to?*

We sometimes put the indirect object at the end of the sentence, where it usually follows the prepositions **to** and **for**.

Jeremy gave the book ***to David****.*

Don't show the answer ***to me****.*

I made a sandwich ***for my sister****.*

1 Replace the underlined words with object pronouns.

1. My brother and I gave <u>a necklace</u> to <u>Mel</u>. My brother and I gave it to her.
2. She gave <u>the book</u> to <u>Stan and Toni</u>. ____________________
3. They gave <u>the book</u> to <u>Tim</u>. ____________________
4. He gave <u>the book</u> to <u>his mother</u>. ____________________
5. She gave <u>the book</u> to <u>my father</u>. ____________________
6. He gave <u>the book</u> to <u>my brother and me</u>. ____________________

2 **Rewrite the sentences with the words in the correct order.**

1 Show / the bracelet, / me / please / . Show me the bracelet, please.

2 Don't / the story / to / tell / Juan / . ______________________

3 You must / the dress / buy / Gabriella / for / . ______________________

4 I gave / the belt / Wang Li / to / . ______________________

5 I bought / Sheila / for / a hat / . ______________________

6 Sarah / me / gave / the necklace / . ______________________

3 **Complete the story with the pronouns *it*, *her*, *them*, *us* and *me*.**

Mr James and the Bag of Sweets

'Give (1) them to (2) ____________, please,' said Mr James.

'But the sweets are Sandra's, Mr James,' said Sonny.

'Yes, I know the sweets are Sandra's, but don't give (3) ____________ back to (4) ____________. It's not break time. You know the rule.'

'Yes, Mr James, I know (5) ____________; you remind (6) ____________ all every day – we mustn't eat sweets in class.'

'Anything,' said Mr James. 'You mustn't eat anything in class. Come on, then. Sandra can have (7) ____________ back at break time.'

I gave Mr James the bag of sweets and sat in my chair. Five minutes later, I looked up from my Maths book.

'Mr James!' I said. 'You're eating (8) ____________. But you said …'

'Yes, I know I did, Sonny,' said Mr James, smiling, 'but they really are very nice sweets.'

Reading: a postcard

1 **Read the postcard, then answer the questions.**

Dear Eve,

Yesterday we went to the fantastic Chocolate Museum. You must go there!

A guide told us all about the history of chocolate and we watched a short film about how to make chocolate. Dad thought the film was great. They had a brilliant collection of old chocolate wrappers, too – Grandma really liked that.

They also gave us some free chocolate to take home. It was delicious!

I hope you are well.

Love
Li Yan

Eve Blackburn
23 January Street
Belfast
Northern Ireland
BT9 5AB

1 Where did Li Yan and her family go?

They went to the Chocolate Museum.

2 What did the guide tell them about?

______

3 Who thought the film was very good?

______

4 Who liked the collection of old chocolate wrappers?

______

5 What did they get to take home?

______

1 Complete the descriptions of the museums with *must* or *mustn't*.

The Football Museum

You (1) ___must___ come to the Football Museum! All fans of the beautiful game (2) ____________ miss it. See the shirt Pelé wore in the 1970 World Cup final. Watch a film about how football began.

The Sword Museum

You (3) ____________ visit us at the Sword Museum! Find out about the history of the sword. See swords of all sizes, from the very, very small to the very, very big. But remember – you (4) ____________ touch the swords!

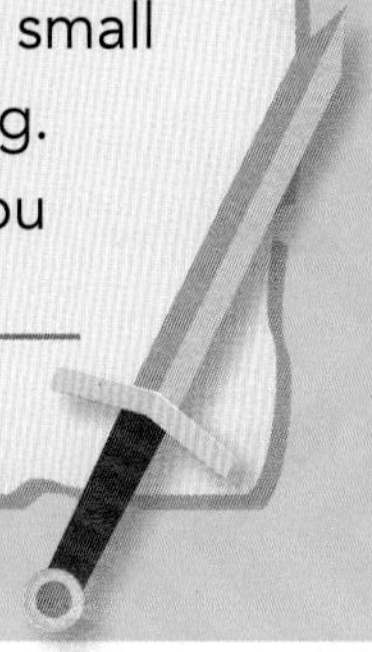

The Royal Museum

The Royal Museum tells the story of Europe's kings and queens. You (5) ____________ ask your History teacher to bring you here. Learn all about the kings of Spain and Harald Fairhair, the first king of Norway.

Help with Writing

We usually write postcards to describe our experiences to friends and family. We often use adjectives such as *brilliant*, *great* and *fantastic* to talk about what we did.

2 Imagine you went to one of the museums in Activity 1. Write a postcard to tell a friend about it. Use Li Yan's postcard on the Reading page to help you.

Listening: exhibits

1 03 **Listen. Are sentences 1–6 true or false?**

Rules at the Shield Museum

1 You must show your ticket to the woman at the door. [t]
2 You can touch some of the shields. [ ]
3 You mustn't take photos of the shields. [ ]
4 You must carry your bag inside the museum. [ ]
5 You can see some shields of famous kings. [ ]
6 You must leave at five o'clock. [ ]

2 04 **Listen to Kasim's story. Complete each sentence with one word.**

1 Kasim and his class visited the Knight __Museum__ yesterday.
2 Kasim's friend William took a ______________ from a shelf and put it on.
3 At the museum, you mustn't touch the helmets, shields or ______________.
4 The woman wasn't happy with Mr Martin because he ______________ in the museum.
5 After the problems, the children didn't touch things, run or ______________.
6 William doesn't want to be a ______________ in the school play.

Speaking

1 Look and write. Then play the description game.

A knight uses this to fight with.

It's a sword!

1 

crown

2 

3 

4 

5 

6 

Help with Speaking

Some words have silent letters. The words *sword* and *knight* have silent letters: you don't pronounce the *w* in *sword* and the *k* and *gh* in *knight*.

2 Work with a friend. Read and talk about the museum rules.

The Museum of Queens and Kings

Remember ...

1 You must show your ticket at the door.
2 You must put your bag in a locker.
3 You mustn't take photos of the exhibits.
4 You mustn't use your mobile phone.
5 You mustn't run or shout.

3 With your friend, write three 'dream rules' for the museum in Activity 2. Then talk about your rules.

Dream rules for the Museum of Queens and Kings

You must ______________________________.
You can ______________________________.
You ______________________________.

You must touch the crowns and bracelets. You can put them on and have fun! You mustn't forget to wear your favourite queen or king costume from our special box.

2 Connectors

Language focus

And, **but**, **so** and **because** are **connectors**. Use them to join two parts of a sentence.

Use **and** and **but** to connect two ideas. Use **but** when the second idea is different to the first. Use a comma before **but**.

We had picnics in the fields ***and*** *we walked through the forest.*
I liked having picnics, ***but*** *I didn't like walking through the forest*

Use **because** and **so** to talk about the reasons for an action. Use a comma before **so**.

I was tired, ***so*** *I went home.* *I went home* ***because*** *I was tired.*

1 Circle the correct connectors to complete the sentences.

1 We went to the village ______________ we climbed the mountain.

a so b and c but

2 We walked by the river, ______________ we didn't swim in it.

a but b because c and

3 We wanted to go on the river, ______________ we took a boat to the island.

a but b and c so

4 We went back to the village early ______________ Mum was sleepy.

a because b and c so

2 Complete the poem with *and*, *so*, *but* or *because*.

The Park Poem

It was a beautiful day,
(1) So we all went to play.
We laughed (2) ______ we joked quite a lot.
We sat in the shade
Of a towering tree
(3) ______ we were hungry and hot.
After sandwiches, chocolate,
Bananas and more,
We were sleepy, (4) ______ then Ricky said,
'I don't know about you,
My two favourite friends,
(5) ______ I think I'm ready for bed.'

3 Complete the sentences with your own ideas.

My Weekend

On Friday, I did my homework and (1) had my dinner. I didn't go to the cinema because (2) ______. On Saturday morning, I was really hungry, so (3) ______. On Saturday afternoon, I went to Dominic's birthday party, but (4) ______. On Sunday morning, it was sunny, so (5) ______. I usually go to my grandparents' house on Sunday afternoons, but last Sunday (6) ______ because ______. On Sunday evening, I watched TV and (7) ______. I went to bed early because (8) ______.

Could / Couldn't

Language focus

Use **could** / **couldn't** to talk about abilities you had or didn't have in the past.

*When she was a girl, she **couldn't** swim, but she **could** ride a bike.*

Yes/No questions are formed in the following way:

***Could** you / he / she / we / they make pancakes?*

*Yes, I / he / she / we / they **could**.*

*No, I / he / she / we / they **couldn't**.*

1 **Answer the questions with *Yes, I could* or *No, I couldn't*.**

1 Could you walk when you were six months old? No, I couldn't.

2 Could you speak when you were one year old? ______

3 Could you run when you were three years old? ______

4 Could you catch a ball when you were four years old? ______

5 Could you read when you were five years old? ______

6 Could you write when you were seven years old? ______

2 Complete the questions with the verbs from the box.

speak play climb ~~run~~ ski ride

www.theoldpeopleswebsite.co.uk

The Old People's Website

When you were a young man …

1 … could you ____run____ fast?
2 … could you ________ mountains?
3 … could you ________ any other languages?
4 … could you ________ the guitar?
5 … could you ________ a motorbike?
6 … could you ________ or snowboard?

3 Match the questions in Activity 2 with the answers.

a No, I couldn't, but my brother could. He was a member of a club. He went up Everest once! [2]

b Yes, I could. I didn't like driving cars, but I loved my second-hand Harley-Davidson! [ ]

c No, I couldn't. I didn't go on winter holidays. They were too expensive! [ ]

d No, I couldn't. I could play the violin, but I didn't learn to play anything else. [ ]

e Yes, I could. I lived in Buenos Aires for five years when I was in my twenties, so my Spanish was very good. [ ]

f Yes, I could. I loved doing that. I used to run by the river near my house every morning. [ ]

Reading: a story

1 **Read the story. Then complete the summary with the words from the box.**

The Strange Tale of Jim Garry's Mountain

It was the mayor who saw it first. 'Another beautiful morning,' he said to himself as he opened his curtains. 'Wait a moment. Jim Garry's Mountain is ...'

It was all the villagers could talk about. 'How can we climb it now?' they asked. Everyone was very worried, so they met in the Town Hall that evening to discuss the problem. 'Thank you all for coming,' said the mayor. 'Now as you know, Jim Garry's mountain is ...'

'It's not just Jim Garry's Mountain,' said a voice.

An old man near the door stood up. His long hair and beard were grey.

'Excuse me,' said the mayor, 'this meeting is for the people of the village only.'

'Don't you want to know what's happening? Why there is no water in the river and no grass in the fields?'

'What are you talking about? We are here to talk about where our mountain went.'

'Everything is going because you don't look after it. You must care for the world around you, Mayor. That is all I want to say. Good evening to you.'

The villagers were more interested in who the man was than what he had to say. Nobody noticed that the forests, fields, lakes and islands were not there any more. The only thing left in the village was the Town Hall and the people in it.

mountain	Town Hall	mayor	people	~~village~~	rivers

One morning, the mayor of the (1) ___village___ finds that the (2) ________ is not there. The (3) ________ of the village are very worried. They have a meeting in the (4) ________. At the meeting, an old man that nobody knows says why everything is going from the village – the trees, the (5) ________, the lakes. The (6) ________ is not very happy with the old man. The old man leaves and the people talk about him. They do not notice what is happening around them.

Writing

1 Match the story types with the definitions.

1 comedy — c
2 history
3 fantasy
4 romance
5 science fiction

a a story about something that happened in the past
b a story about things that aren't real or things that can't happen, e.g. a story in which people can fly
c a story that makes you laugh
d a story about technology, the future and space
e a story about people who fall in love

Help with Writing

Try to make your readers interested in your story. One way to do this is to give them a question they want to find the answer to. For example, the opening sentence of 'The Strange Tale of Jim Garry's Mountain' is 'It was the mayor who saw it first.' The writer doesn't tell us what 'it' is, so we want to read on to find out.

2 You are going to write a short story about something strange that happens in a village. You must write it in the past simple. Before you write your story, plan it by making notes about the following:

- The type of story (e.g. science fiction, fantasy).
- The characters.
- The plot.

3 Now write your short story. Use 'The Strange Tale of Jim Garry's Mountain' and your notes from Activity 2 to help you.

Listening: places

1 (05) **Listen and put Ana's story in order.**

- [ ] They walked on a long path through a forest.
- [ ] Ana took lots of photos.
- [ ] It started to rain.
- [1] Last weekend, Ana went to the countryside with her parents.
- [ ] Ana and her parents had a picnic.
- [ ] They climbed up a mountain.
- [ ] Ana and her parents had cake in a café.

2 (06) **What could Leo do when he was six? Listen and tick ✓ or cross ✗.**

Speaking

1 **Look at these places and imagine you went there. Play the guessing game.**

I was in town. I wanted to look at comics, so …

You went to a bookshop! I was outdoors. I wanted to swim, so …

You went to a lake!

bookshop

lake

café

cinema

mountain

forest

2 **Look at Activity 1 and choose a place that you went to. Write answers. Then practise.**

1 Where did you go?

____

2 Who did you go with?

____

3 How did you get there?

____

4 Why did you go there?

____

5 What did you do and see?

____

3 **Talk about your place.**

Last weekend, I went to a lake with my family. We got there by train. We went there because we love being in the countryside. We walked around the lake and then we swam in it. We saw some big fish and beautiful birds!

3 Past continuous

Language focus

Use the **past continuous** to talk about events that were happening at a particular moment in the past, e.g.
*Onur **was climbing** a mountain.*

Form the past continuous with **was** / **were** + **verb** + **ing**:

*I / he / she **was watching** a TV programme about firefighters.*

*We / you / they **were playing** football in the garden.*

1 **Circle the correct verb forms to complete the text.**

On Saturday afternoon, everyone (1) *was* / *were* doing something. My brother Pablo (2) *was* / *were* reading about the Great Fire of London. My parents (3) *was* / *were* cleaning the kitchen. My sister Lucia (4) *was* / *were* playing a computer game called *Emergency!* My cousins Maria and Gonzalo (5) *was* / *were* painting. I (6) *was* / *were* doing something too. Can you guess what it was? Yes, that's right! I (7) *was* / *were* watching what everyone else was doing!

2 Match 1–6 with a–f.

1 I was
2 My brother was
3 My grandparents were
4 My sisters were in
5 My dog was
6 Sarah, my best friend, was

a chasing the cat round the garden. That's her favourite thing to do.
b at home watching a TV programme about the emergency services. Grandma said it was very interesting.
c making a web page on the internet. She's very good with technology.
d the kitchen, making their favourite type of pizza: bananas and onion. Ugh!
e sleeping. He's always tired. He works really hard in school.
f doing my Science homework. I didn't enjoy doing it because it was really hard!

3 Correct the verbs in sentences 1–5. Make past continuous sentences.

1 The firefighters were climb the ladder.
The firefighters were climbing the ladder.
2 The police officers were ran very quickly.
____
3 Sara was make a sandwich.
____
4 The paramedic were working very hard.
____
5 My friends was watching a film about a flood.
____

4 Complete the sentences so they are true for you.

1 On Saturday morning, I _______________.
2 On Saturday afternoon, my parents _______________.
3 On Saturday evening, my family _______________.
4 On Sunday morning, I _______________.
5 On Sunday afternoon, my friends and I _______________.
6 On Sunday evening, I _______________.

Past continuous questions

Language focus

Use **past continuous questions** to ask someone what they were doing at a particular moment in the past, e.g.

I rang you at six. You didn't answer. Were you washing up?

Yes/No questions are formed with **was** / **were** + **verb** + **ing**, e.g.

Were *we / they sleep**ing** last night?*	*Yes, we / they were.*	*No, we / they weren't.*
Was *he / she do**ing** his homework?*	*Yes, he / she was.*	*No, he / she wasn't.*

'Wh' questions are formed by putting **where**, **what**, **why**, etc., before **was** / ***were*** + **verb** + **ing**, e.g.

What *book **were** you **reading**?*	*I was reading one about history.*
Where were *your friends **going**?*	*They were going to the park to play tennis.*

1 **Rewrite the questions with the words in the correct order.**

1 you / were / what / yesterday / doing / ? What were you doing yesterday?

2 you / were / sleeping / ? ______

3 what / friend / doing / was / your / ? ______

4 was / book / she / reading / a / ? ______

5 going / you / were / where / ? ______

6 at / brother / three / doing / your / was / what / o'clock / ? ______

2 **Complete the questions with *was* / *were* and the verbs from the box in the correct form. Then write the answers.**

play drink read run sit clean ~~eat~~

1 Was the man in the blue T-shirt cleaning the window? Yes, he was.
2 __________ the man in a red T-shirt __________ a pizza? __________
3 __________ the two women __________ water? __________
4 __________ the woman in the red dress __________ down? __________
5 __________ the police officer __________ after a man? __________
6 __________ the man with glasses __________ a book? __________

3 **Complete the questions.**

1 What / you / do / four o'clock / afternoon / Monday?
What were you doing at four o'clock in the afternoon on Monday?
2 What / you / do / six o'clock / morning / Wednesday?
____
3 What / you / do / five o'clock / afternoon / Friday?
____
4 What / you / do / nine o'clock / evening / Saturday?
____
5 What / you / do / six o'clock / morning / Sunday?
____

Reading: an email

1 Read the email, then answer the questions.

To grannyandgranpa@oldpeopleemail.com

Subject The Great Flood Of Calle Dos Santos

Hi, Granny

I've got some news – we had an accident today.
Don't worry, everyone is all right. Mum is going to call you later.

It happened yesterday afternoon. We were in Calle Dos Santos, on our way to the cinema. Suddenly, we noticed that there was water ahead of us on the road. It was coming into the car! It all happened so quickly. One minute we were driving along, and then … 'Everyone out!' said Dad. We got out, but Dad caught his leg on the door. We called the emergency services. The police were the first to arrive. The firefighters came next because there were lots of cars that were stuck. They had to pull them out. Then the paramedics came. 'You must keep your leg still,' said one of them to Dad. His leg was really hurting him, but it wasn't broken. The paramedics gave us special emergency blankets to keep warm. I really liked wearing mine and asked if I could take it home.

I've got to go now, Granny. Dad can't walk very well at the moment, so he wants me to go to the kitchen and make him a cup of tea.

Email soon with all your news!

Love,
Valentina

1 When did the accident happen? It happened yesterday afternoon.
2 Where were Valentina and her parents going? ______
3 What happened? ______
4 What did Valentina's dad hurt? ______
5 Who arrived after the police officers? ______
6 What did they give Valentina's family? ______

1 Write the phrases from the box in the correct part of the table.

Bye for now   Hi ______   Dear ______
Email me soon   Best wishes   How are you?
Hello ______   Is everything OK?   How are things?

Starting an email	
Asking how someone is	
Finishing an email	

Help with Writing

When you tell someone your news in an email, give them the important information, but do not write too much.

2 You are going to write an email to Valentina telling her all about a fire in a local café. Before you write, make notes about the following:

- When and where the fire started.
- What you were doing when it started.
- What the firefighters said and did.

To: valentina@hispanomail.com   Subject: The fire in the café

Hello, Valentina

Thanks for your email! ______

______

______

______

Send me another email soon!

Love,

______

Listening: emergency, emergency!

1 07 **Listen to Jack's story and write *t* (true) or *f* (false).**

1 Jack, Lea and John went to a park last Sunday. [t]
2 They climbed the tallest tree in the park. [ ]
3 The children got to the top of the tree, and it wasn't raining. [ ]
4 There was a storm and a flood, so the children couldn't climb down the tree. [ ]
5 Jack phoned his parents and the emergency services. [ ]
6 A firefighter helped the children to come down from the tree. [ ]

2 08 **Listen to the conversations. Circle the correct answers.**

1 What was Theo doing yesterday at three o'clock?
a He was reading a book. (b) He was watching a film.
2 Was Amy watching TV yesterday at four o'clock?
a Yes, she was. b No, she wasn't.
3 How was Jamie yesterday?
a He wasn't feeling well. b He was feeling OK.
4 Who forgot to do the homework?
a Eva. b Harry.
5 What was Freddie doing before twelve o'clock yesterday?
a He was sleeping. b He was having breakfast.
6 Where was it raining this morning?
a In the village near the beach. b At the beach.

1 **Work with a friend. Look at the pictures and tell the story. Use the words, and the past simple and past continuous.**

Yesterday, it was a warm day. The sun was shining and …

warm day / sun shine / children do some work

fire alarm ring / fire

children and teacher go to playground / room at the top on fire

firefighters arrive / everything OK

2 **Choose one of the photos. Imagine you work for the emergency services. How did you help the animal? Write answers. Then practise.**

1 What's your job?

____

2 What happened?

____

3 What was the animal doing?

____

4 How did you help the animal?

____

3 **Tell your story from Activity 2.**

I'm a police officer. Last Monday, it rained all day and there was a flood. I was driving my police car and saw a dog on a roof. The dog was …

4 at / in / on

Language focus

At, **in** and **on** are **prepositions**. Use them to talk about days, dates, times of the day, periods of time or when things take place, e.g.

*I was born **at** nine o'clock in the morning in December.*

Use **at** with a point of time and the word **night**.

*We're going to the cinema **at** six o'clock.*
*My brother can't sleep **at** night.*

Use **in** with months of the year, seasons, years, and the phrases **the morning** and **the afternoon**.

*My sister's birthday is **in** summer, **in** July.*
*I was born **in** 2011.*
*What did you do **in** the afternoon?*

Use **on** with days of the week and with **morning**, **afternoon**, **evening** and **night** when you put the day before those words.

*We've got a History test **on** Wednesday.*
*What time does the bus leave **on** Saturday morning?*

1 **Complete the sentences with *in*, *on* or *at*.**

1 Is your birthday ____in____ June?
2 That film you want to see starts ________ six o'clock.
3 We're all going to the beach ________ Saturday.
4 We went to my cousins' house ________ Sunday afternoon.
5 What time do you go to bed ________ night?
6 The train leaves at four o'clock ________ the afternoon.

2 **Correct the sentences.**

1 My birthday is on October.

My birthday is in October.

2 The film starts in seven o'clock.

____

3 We went swimming in the sea on the morning.

____

4 My uncle and aunt came to our house for dinner at Sunday.

____

5 Did you see Sean at Tuesday?

____

6 We're going to the park in Saturday afternoon.

____

3 **Match 1–10 with a–j.**

1 Did your sister move to Barcelona in — c
2 The dog next door to us always barks
3 What did you do
4 I'd like to go to the beach
5 Is your birthday in
6 Does the bus leave
7 I usually go to bed
8 My friends and I love to have picnics
9 My grandparents always have lunch
10 I do my homework in

a in summer. Our favourite spot is next to the river.
b on Saturday. It's going to be hot!
c 2012 or 2013?
d at 4.00 or does it go at 4.15?
e the afternoon when I come home from school.
f November or December? Mine is in January.
g at 9.30 in the week. I need lots of sleep!
h at exactly one o'clock in the afternoon.
i in the morning? Did you go swimming?
j at night. Sometimes, I can't sleep. It's very noisy!

Past continuous and past simple

Language focus

Use **past continuous** and **past simple** together to talk about one action interrupting another in the past.

When you describe two actions using these tenses, you can order the sentence in two ways. You can put the past continuous action first followed by the **past simple**:

I was doing my homework when my computer broke.

You can also put the **past simple** first followed by the **past continuous**. When you write the sentence in this way, use a comma.

When my computer broke, I was doing my homework.

1 **Complete the sentences with the correct form of the verbs from the box. Use either the past continuous or past simple.**

meet	play	~~wait~~	do	fall	begin

1 I was waiting for the train when I saw my friend.

2 When my brother came home, I ________ my homework.

3 We were playing football when it ________ to snow.

4 Mum was living in Ankara when she ________ Dad.

5 My brother ________ basketball when he broke his leg.

6 My sister was doing her Geography homework when she ________ asleep.

2 Circle the correct words to complete the sentences.

1 When I *bumped* / *was bumping* into the tree, I was running after the football.

2 I *watched* / *was watching* TV when you called me.

3 When we *were seeing* / *saw* Miss Gunn, the History teacher, we were waiting for a train.

4 We *were sunbathing* / *sunbathed* when it started to rain. We ran into a café nearby to stay dry!

5 My dad was walking down the street when he *was finding* / *found* the bag.

6 My brother was making a salad for lunch when he *cut* / *was cutting* his finger.

3 Write the underlined verbs in the story in the past simple or past continuous.

I (1) am walking through the park on my way home from town when I (2) see a large bear standing in front of me. It (3) is playing the violin. 'Good afternoon,' (4) says the bear. 'Oh,' I (5) say, 'good afternoon.' I (6) am thinking of starting to run when the bear (7) says, 'I'm not a real bear, you know. This is just a special suit. I'm playing at a children's party later.' The bear (8) wants to do a bit of practice before the show. I (9) listen for a while. She (10) isn't bad, for a bear.

1 was walking
2 ______
3 ______
4 ______
5 ______
6 ______
7 ______
8 ______
9 ______
10 ______

Reading: a newspaper article

1 **Read the newspaper article, then answer the questions.**

The Globe

5th March

Dog Rolls Down Escalator

There was great excitement at King's Cross railway station this morning when a small dog rolled all the way down an escalator. Cuddles, a three-year-old Yorkshire terrier belonging to Mrs Cynthia Bolton, 48, of Newcastle, wasn't hurt, but his owner was shocked.

Mrs Bolton said, 'We bought our tickets at the ticket office and then walked to the escalator. Cuddles and I were standing at the top of it when I heard the announcer make his announcement: 'The train now arriving at Platform 4 is the 9.52 to Glasgow.' 'Quick!' I said to Cuddles. 'That's our train!' I ran forward, slipped on a bit of paper on the floor and dropped the dog. Cuddles rolled all the way down the escalator, landing in a rucksack at the bottom. Before I knew what was happening, I saw a man pick up the rucksack – with Cuddles inside – and walk onto the train. 'Stop!' I shouted. 'That man's got my Cuddles!'

Other passengers were also surprised. 'We were walking up the stairs,' said John Maloney.

'What happened was just amazing! We put our suitcases down and stopped where we were. We wanted to see what was going on.'

Mrs Bolton didn't think twice. She ran down the escalator as fast she could, jumped onto the train, found the passenger and managed to get her dog back. Cuddles was fine and the pair made their journey home.

1 How old is Mrs Bolton? 48.

2 What platform did the announcer talk about? ______

3 What was Mrs Bolton doing when she heard the announcement? ______

______

4 What did Mrs Bolton slip on? ______

5 What did Cuddles fall into? ______

1 Complete the table with the information from the box.

'It was terrible. They walked on without paying for a ticket.'
'Everyone must pay to use the service. The rules are for everyone.'
Two boys got onto a train without a ticket.
The transport police asked the boys to get off the train.
On Platform 3 at Liverpool Street Station in London.

What happened	
Where it happened	
What people said	
What happened in the end	

Help with Writing

Newspaper articles often include things that people said about the story. Reporters add these to make their articles more interesting for the reader.

2 Imagine you write for a newspaper. Write an article about what happened at Liverpool Street Station. Use the information in Activity 1 and the newspaper article about Cuddles to help you. Include:

- A title for the article.
- The names of the two boys.
- Where they wanted to go.
- The names of the other people in Activity 1.

Listening: tickets, please!

1 09 **Listen to the conversation. Answer the questions.**

1 Where does Samuel want to go?

He wants to go to Cambridge.

2 How many tickets does Samuel buy?

____

3 What is Samuel's mum doing?

____

4 How much does Samuel pay for the tickets?

____

5 Which platform does the train leave from?

____

6 When does the next train leave?

____

2 10 **Listen to Diana's story. Complete the sentences.**

1 Every year, Diana and her dad watch a theatre play in London.

2 Last Saturday morning, Diana and her dad were at the _______ _______.

3 Diana's dad bought a _______ of _______ and some apple juice there.

4 When the train arrived at _______ 1, Diana's dad was feeling worried.

5 Diana's dad couldn't find the _______ for the theatre.

6 When Diana and her dad got to the theatre, lots of people were waiting in front of the _______ _______.

7 The man at the desk gave the _______ to Diana's dad.

8 Diana and her dad walked up the _______ to get to their seats. They loved the play.

Speaking

1 **Look at the departures board. Play the guessing game.**

It leaves from Platform 1.

When does it leave?

It leaves at half past eleven.

It's the train to Cardiff!

Departures

City	Platform	Time
Oxford	3	11:00
Cambridge	5	11:00
Cardiff	1	11:30
Glasgow	4	11:30
Manchester	4	12:15
London	5	12:15
Liverpool	3	1:45
Leeds	1	1:45

2 **Draw a departures board with four cities from your country. Talk about your board.**

The train to Córdoba leaves from Platform 3. It leaves at quarter past two.

Help with Speaking

When you buy things, don't forget to say please and thank you to the shop assistant. It is good to be polite!

3 **Work with a friend. Use each other's departures boards. Buy tickets.**

Hello. Can I have a ticket to Córdoba, please?

Yes, of course. Single or return?

Single. How much is that?

That's twelve euros, please.

Here you are.

Thanks. Here's your ticket.

Thank you very much.

5 Used to

Language focus

Use **used to** to talk about things you did routinely in the past or the way things were in the past, e.g.

*My grandmother **used to** be a teacher. She **used to** teach Spanish.*

When we use **used to**, we are saying that things are different now:

*My sister **used to** play the piano. (She doesn't play it now.)*

*My brother **used to** draw cartoons. (He doesn't draw them now.)*

1 Complete the sentences with the verbs from the box.

be ~~have~~ live play work make

www.thewebsite.com

The other day, I was thinking about how things change. For example, I used to (1) ____have____ blonde hair when I was younger. It's dark now. My friends and I used to (2) ________ football every Saturday morning, but these days we never do that. I used to (3) ________ with my parents and brother in a small flat in the centre of our city, but now we live in a big house with a garden in a village outside the city. Dad used to (4) ________ for a newspaper, but now he works for a website. Mum used to (5) ________ a children's television programme called *Milkshake*, but now she writes stories. Grandad used to (6) ________ a police officer, but now he is retired. Nothing stays the same. It can be sad sometimes, but it keeps things interesting!

2 **Are the sentences correct or incorrect? Correct the sentences you think are incorrect.**

1 David use to carry a walkie-talkie.

Incorrect. David used to carry a walkie-talkie.

2 Tina used to interview suspects.

______ ____________________

3 Brian used to work in a police station.

______ ____________________

4 Jerry used to wearing a uniform.

______ ____________________

5 Chris using to catch criminals.

______ ____________________

6 Jonathan used drive a fast car.

______ ____________________

3 **Write sentences with *used to*. Then write what the person does or has now.**

1 Ceren used to play basketball.
Now she plays tennis.

2 Sandro ____________________
____

3 Elena ____________________
____

4 Sam ____________________
____

Had to

Language focus

Use **had to** to talk about something that someone told you to do, e.g. *Dad **had to** paint the fence at the weekend. Mum told him it was looking a bit dirty.*

1 Rewrite the sentences with the words in the correct order.

1 rooms / tidy / we/ to / had / our — We had to tidy our rooms.

2 had / homework / to / his / Dom / do — ______

3 to / wash / dishes / had / the / Marlene / up — ______

4 had / clean / to / the / Sofia / windows — ______

5 Neil / sweep / floor / had / the / to — ______

6 walk / dog / had / Ada / to / the — ______

7 cook / had/ Pablo / to / meal / the / evening — ______

8 early / bed / had / Zehra / to / to / go — ______

2 Circle the correct verb forms to complete the text.

My brother went to a police academy last year. Things weren't easy there! Lessons used to (1) *start* / *starting* at 6.00. They had to (2) *wore* / *wear* a uniform. They had to (3) *go* / *goes* running every day. They had to (4) *spent* / *spend* two hours every evening doing homework. They had to (5) *did* / *do* tests about how to be a police officer every Monday morning. Oh, and they had to (6) *attend* / *attending* on Saturday mornings too! He enjoyed it, but he's happy he doesn't have to go there now.

3 Look at the pictures. Then write sentences using *had to* and the verbs from the box.

cook dinner ~~do the shopping~~
study for an exam take wash up
clean the bathroom

1 Mick had to do the shopping for his grandma.

2 Marco ______________________ for his family.

3 Mia ______________________ at the weekend.

4 Pedro ______________________ after dinner.

5 Stephanie ______________________ before she could watch TV.

6 Katya ______________________ her little sister to school.

Reading: a description

1 **Read the blog post, then complete the sentences.**

Lou's blog about school

9th March

Describing Detectives

We had a really interesting class this morning. We talked about detectives. Detectives are a special type of police officer. Their job is to investigate serious crimes like murder. 'My sister used to be a detective,' said Mr Garcia. 'Wow!' I said. 'Did she enjoy the job?' 'Yes, she did,' said Mr Garcia, 'but it wasn't easy.' Then he told us all about his sister's job. She used to work at night and used to work long hours. She had to look for clues. She had to interview suspects. She had to work really hard to solve the murders.

Later, Mr Garcia asked us to describe a detective. But he didn't want us to describe a real detective – we had to invent one. We had to give our detective a name and describe his or her daily life. I called my detective Inspector Bach. This was my description of him: Inspector Bach didn't have any hair, but he had a beard and moustache. There was a scar on the end of his nose. He liked to touch the scar. Inspector Bach used to work on solving murders. He used to solve his crimes in an unusual way: by listening to music. 'I always get my best ideas then,' he said. Inspector Bach used to work on his own. 'I like to be quiet,' he said. 'It helps me think.'

(10 comments)

1 Mr Garcia's sister used to be a ___detective___.
2 Mr Garcia's sister ________ for clues.
3 Mr Garcia asked Lou's class to invent their own ________.
4 Lou called his detective ________.
5 Lou's detective ________ his crimes by listening to music.

1 **Describe members of your family. Use the words from the box.**

beard	moustache	blonde	fair	dark	curly	straight	long	short

1 ______________________________

2 ______________________________

3 ______________________________

4 ______________________________

5 ______________________________

Help with Writing

When you write a description of someone, you want the reader to imagine what they look like. You can do this by using interesting details. For example, Lou tells us that Inspector Bach had a scar on the end of his nose.

2 **Invent your own detective. Write a description of him or her. Use Lou's description of Inspector Bach to help you. Include:**

- Your detective's name.
- A description of his or her hair, eyes, height, etc.
- The things your detective used to do and had to do.

My detective: 6th January

Listening: officers and criminals

1 (11) **Listen and write *t* (true) or *f* (false).**

1 Kelly and her mum had to buy a present for Kelly's dad. [t]
2 Kelly's dad used to be a journalist, but he isn't now. [ ]
3 Kelly was with her mum in a new pen shop called Write Now. [ ]
4 There was a clothes shop where the pen shop is now. [ ]
5 A woman was stealing some notebooks in the pen shop. [ ]
6 The woman was blonde and there was a scar on her cheek. [ ]
7 Kelly's mum phoned the police. [ ]
8 The police couldn't catch the woman. [ ]

2 (12) **Listen to Max talk about his aunt. Put the sentences in order.**

[ ] Max's aunt worked as a police officer for ten years.
[1] Max's Aunt Vicky was a police officer before she was a photographer.
[ ] She had to be careful and she used to work all night.
[ ] Auntie Vicky hasn't got straight dark hair now.
[ ] She had to wear a uniform and she used to carry a walkie-talkie.
[ ] Max's aunt chased and caught criminals.

1 Work with a friend. Read the news report. Then choose your questions and ask and answer.

www.dailynews.nex   Search GO!

Robbery at Bank

There was a robbery at the North Bank. It was on Saturday afternoon at 3 p.m. The robber stole thousands of pounds and some important documents. The police are looking for a young man. He is about 30 years old. He has got short dark hair, a beard and a moustache. The man has got blue eyes and there is a scar above his right eye. Please call the Central Police Station with any information.

Student A

Where and when was the robbery?
How old is the robber?
What has the robber got above one of his eyes?

Student B

What did the robber steal?
Can you describe the robber?
Who should you give any information to?

2 With your friend, look at the suspects for the bank robbery. Can you describe them?

Can you describe George Nash?

He's got short dark hair …

a George Nash

b Liam Walton

c Jordan Thomas

3 Talk to your friend. Which of the suspects robbed the bank? Why do you think this?

I think … robbed the bank because he …

6 Comparatives and superlatives

Language focus

Use **comparatives** to compare two people, places or things, e.g. *Josep is faster than Marco.*

There are some rules to learn:

Add **-er** to the end of adjectives with one syllable, e.g. **slower**.

Put **more** before adjectives of two or more syllables, e.g. **more difficult**.

There are some irregular forms, e.g. **better**, **worse**.

Use **superlatives** to say one thing or person in a group has the most of a particular quality, e.g. *Josep is* ***the fastest runner*** *I know.*

Add **-est** to the end of adjectives with one syllable, e.g. **slowest**.

Put **the most** before adjectives of two or more syllables, e.g. **the most difficult**.

There are some irregular forms, e.g. **the best**, **the worst**.

1 **Write the comparatives and the superlatives.**

1 big	bigger	the biggest
2 strong	______	______
3 heavy	______	______
4 friendly	______	______
5 dangerous	______	______
6 beautiful	______	______

2 Rewrite the sentences with the words in the correct order.

1 lions / are / smaller / domestic / than / much / cats / .

Domestic cats are much smaller than lions.

2 in / biggest / world / some / the / are / animals / elephants / the / of / .

____

3 interesting / beasts / are / than / real / more / mythical / animals / .

____

4 are / dangerous/ the / Africa / mosquitos / animals / in / most / ?

____

5 fastest / cheetah / animal / the / the / land / is / .

____

6 necks / kangaroos / than / giraffes / longer / have / .

____

3 Complete the text with the comparative or superlative form of the adjectives.

My parents gave me a great present for my birthday – *The Dictionary of Mythical Beasts*. It is the (1) most interesting (interesting) book I know. It taught me about unicorns, Pegasus and the Sphinx. I read it every morning before breakfast and every night before I fall asleep. One evening, after dinner, I couldn't find it anywhere. 'Oh no!' I said. 'This is (2) ______________ (bad) day of my life! Where is my book, Fred? Help me!' But my brother was too busy playing *The Phoenix Rises*, his new video game. 'This is much (3) ______________ (exciting) than your old book,' he said. 'No, it's not,' I said. 'My book teaches me things. Your game is just for fun.' 'But when I play this,' said Fred, 'I learn how to see things that move quickly. I see them (4) ______________ (good) than I did before. This morning, for example, I saw Roger running really fast into the garden.' Roger is our dog. 'He had something in his mouth. It looked (5) ______________ (heavy) than his toy bones. I took it from him before up he could chew it. Have a look over there.' I found my book in Roger's basket. On its cover were marks from Roger's teeth, but it was OK. 'Thanks, Fred,' I said. 'You're (6) ______________ (good) brother in the world! Can you show me how to play *The Phoenix Rises*?'

It looks like ...

Language focus

Use **it looks like** to talk about the appearance of someone or something, e.g. *Unicorns* ***look like*** *horses.*

The phrase is used to ask about someone or something's appearance.

What does your brother ***look like****? He's tall and has got short black hair.*

Note that **looks like** is not used in the reply.

It's also used to compare appearances.

Who does your sister ***look like****? She* ***looks like*** *my mum.*

Look at that cloud! It ***looks like*** *a face.*

1 Correct the sentences.

1 Who are your brother look like?

Who does your brother look like?

2 Who do you looking like?

____

3 Does a centaur looks like a man?

____

4 What do mermaids look liking?

____

2 **Match the answers with the questions in Activity 1.**

a Well, I've got short black hair and brown eyes. I look like my dad. ☐

b He looks a little bit like my mum. They've both got long noses. [1]

c Yes and no. They've got the head and body of a man but the legs of a horse. ☐

d They look like women, but with fish tails instead of legs. ☐

3 **Complete the description with the words from the box.**

like it looks does ~~look~~

The Dictionary of Mythical Beasts

L is for the Loch Ness Monster

What do mythical creatures (1) ___look___ like? Well, they are all different. It depends on the imagination of their creators. The Loch Ness Monster is the most famous mythical beast of the United Kingdom. People come from all over the world, hoping to see this creature swimming about in a large lake in the Highlands of Scotland.

What (2) ________ it look like? Nobody knows, of course, but some people who believe it exists say that it (3) ________ like a dinosaur while others say (4) ________ looks like a dragon. It's got a long neck and a small head. Have a look at the picture. What do you think it looks (5) ________?

Reading: a description of an animal

1 **Read about the babirusa, then complete descriptions a–e with words from the box.**

The Babirusa

The babirusa is not the most famous animal in the world, but it is certainly one of the most interesting. The word 'babirusa' itself is Malay and means 'pig-deer', although the animals look more like pigs than deer. These wild pigs live in the forests of Indonesia and are endangered – there are fewer than 10,000 of them left.

There are four species of babirusa. The most well known of the species are brown or grey in colour and have tails up to 32 centimetres in length. They eat fruit, grasses and leaves as well as other small animals. The males are larger than the females. Like elephants and walruses, these animals have large teeth that come out of their mouths. But babirusas are unusual. The upper tusks of the males come out of their snouts, not their mouths. They look like horns.

deer	~~tusks~~	walrus	forest	snout

a A set of large pointed teeth, like those of an elephant. *tusks*

b An animal that moves fast. The males have horns called antlers. ____________

c A large area of land covered with trees. ____________

d The nose of an animal, especially that of a pig. ____________

e An animal that lives in and around the sea at the North Pole. It has thick skin and two long tusks. ____________

1 **Complete the table with the information from the box.**

The rainforests of Madagascar | Aye-aye
Is nocturnal, so sleeps in the day
Insects and fruit | Spends its life in trees
Has got big eyes and ears and a tail longer than its body
Doesn't look like a primate but is related to apes, chimps and humans

Name	
Where it lives	
What it looks like	
How it lives	
What it eats	

2 **Write about the aye-aye. Use the information in the table in Activity 1 and the description of the babirusa to help you.**

Help with Writing

A short description of an animal should give as much information as possible in a few words. Try to answer possible questions in your description, e.g. *How big is it? How long does it live?*

Listening: the Terrible Omnix

1 13 **Listen and number the pictures in the correct order.**

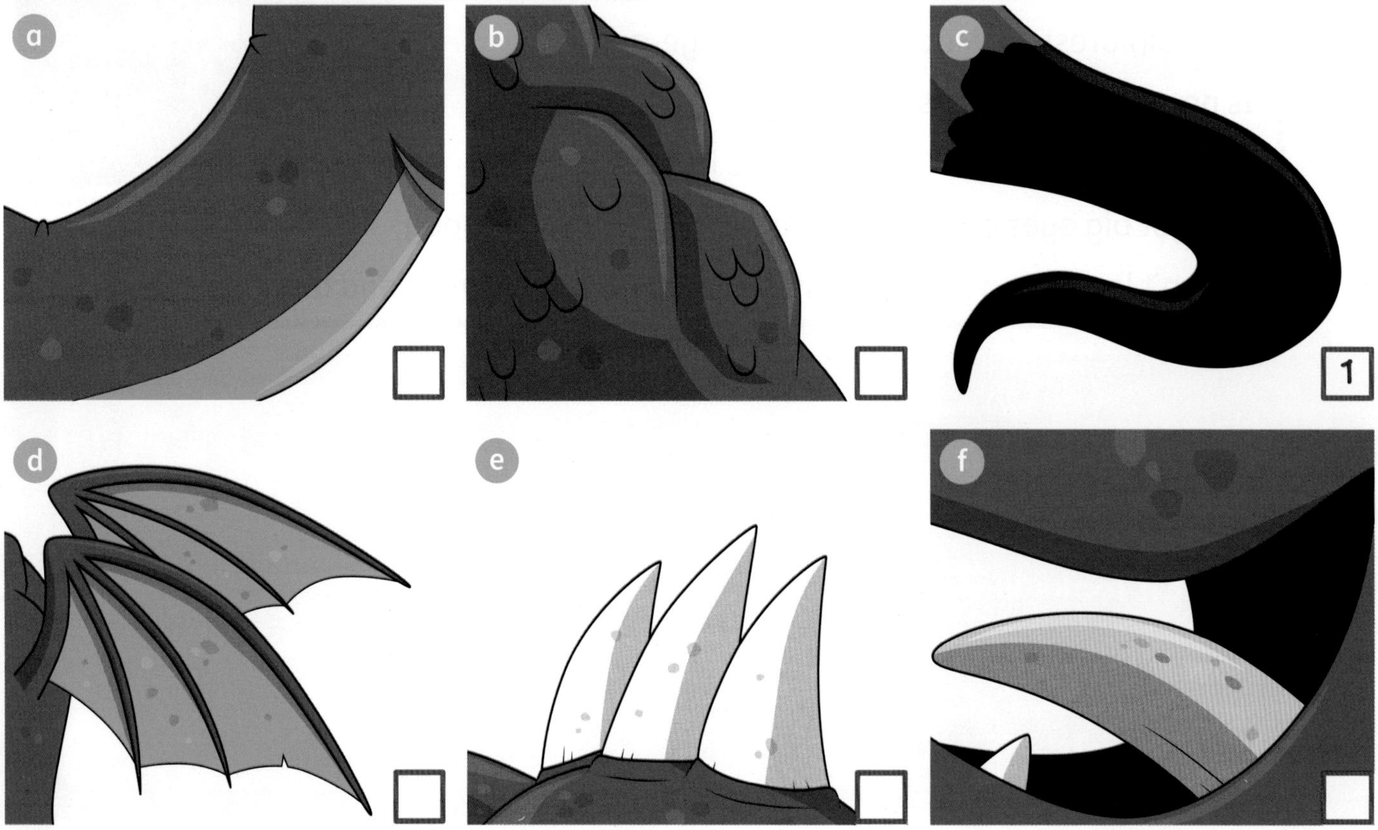

2 14 **Listen to the conversation. Circle the correct words.**

1 Edward / *Laura* is reading *The Terrible Omnix*.

2 The Trussock and the *Munkle* / *Arkle* look like crocodiles.

3 The smallest beast in the forest looks like a *monkey* / *dragon*.

4 The Galloping Runnyback is *Edward's* / *Laura's* favourite beast.

5 The Ginocat is *more beautiful* / *uglier* that the Galloping Runnyback.

6 The Gagger is *faster* / *slower* than the Ginocat.

7 The Gagger looks like a *stegosaurus* / *T-Rex*.

1 **Look at the advertisement. Write answers. Then practise.**

A new beast for Maya's forest!

The author of *The Terrible Omnix*, Susie Lewis, is looking for a new beast for Maya's adventures. Can you think of one? Answer the questions and send your ideas to theterribleomnix@fantasybooks.co.uk. Good luck!

1 What's your beast's name?

____

2 Where in the forest does the beast live?

____

3 What does the beast look like?

____

4 What can it do?

____

5 Who are the beast's friends?

____

2 **Work with a friend. Talk about your beast. Ask and answer the questions in Activity 1.**

What's your beast's name?

It's called the Giant Flapalot. What's your beast's name?

It's called the Birdix.

3 **Work with another friend. Tell them about your friend's beast from Activity 2.**

Luke's beast is called the Birdix. It lives in the biggest tree in the forest. It looks like a bird, but it has got four wings. It can fly very fast. Its friends are the Munkle and the Ginocat.

7 Possessive pronouns

Language focus

Use **possessive pronouns** to talk about things that belong to you, e.g. *Is this Jon's case? No, it's* ***mine****.*

Possessive adjective		**Possessive pronoun**	
my	*your*	*mine*	*yours*
his	*her*	*his*	*hers*
our	*their*	*ours*	*theirs*

1 Circle the correct words to complete the sentences.

1 Is this Leo's coat?
Yes, it's *hers* / *his*.

2 Look! These are *his* / *our* scooters!
Yes! That's mine and that's yours, Antonio!

3 Is that her violin?
No, it's not. *Hers* / *Mine* is over there.

4 These aren't my pencils. Are they *yours* / *hers?*
No, they're not mine.

5 Are you sure this violin is Tom and Deb's?
Yes, it's *theirs* / *ours.* I saw them with it earlier.

6 Is that the guitar you parents got you for your birthday?
No, it isn't. *Mine* / *Yours* is at home.

2 **Rewrite the sentences with possessive pronouns.**

1 It's my tractor. It's mine.
2 Is that your car? ____________
3 That's his book. ____________
4 It's her keyboard. ____________
5 These are our instruments. ____________
6 Are these their bags? ____________

3 **Replace the underlined words with possessive pronouns.**

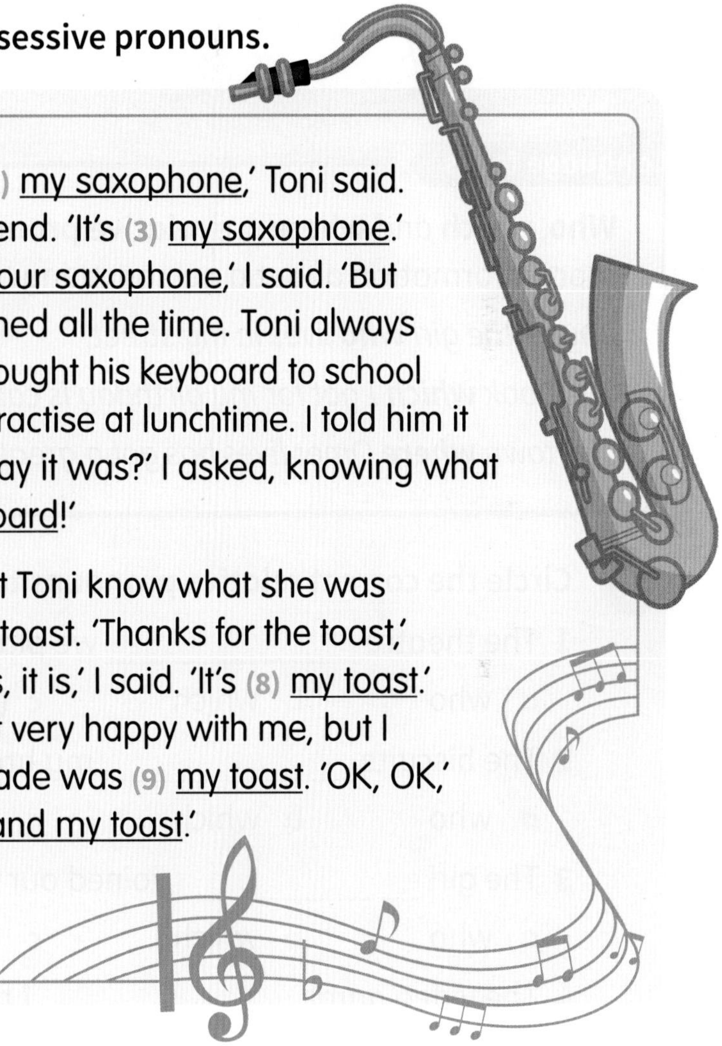

It was my saxophone, not Toni's. 'This is (1) my saxophone,' Toni said. 'It's not (2) her saxophone,' I said to my friend. 'It's (3) my saxophone.' Toni had her own saxophone. 'That's (4) your saxophone,' I said. 'But I don't like that one,' she said. This happened all the time. Toni always wanted what other people had. 'Harry brought his keyboard to school today,' she told me once. 'He wanted to practise at lunchtime. I told him it wasn't (5) his keyboard.' 'Whose did you say it was?' I asked, knowing what the answer was going to be. '(6) My keyboard!'

One morning, at breakfast, I decided to let Toni know what she was like. She sat down at the table with some toast. 'Thanks for the toast,' I said. 'It's not (7) your toast,' she said. 'Yes, it is,' I said. 'It's (8) my toast.' I did this every day for a week. She wasn't very happy with me, but I didn't stop saying that all the toast she made was (9) my toast. 'OK, OK,' she said a week later. 'It's (10) your toast and my toast.'

1 mine
2 ____________
3 ____________
4 ____________
5 ____________
6 ____________
7 ____________
8 ____________
9 ____________
10 ____________

who / which / where

Language focus

Who, **which** and **where** are **relative pronouns**. Use these words to give more information about a person, thing or place.

Anya's the girl ***who*** *lives in my street.*

The book ***which*** *I got for my birthday is called* How To Play The Guitar.

The town ***where*** *Omer lives has got a great new cinema.*

1 Circle the correct relative pronouns to complete the sentences.

1 The theatre ______________ we played our first concert is the oldest in our town.
   a who   b which   c where

2 The biscuits ______________ my brother and sister made are delicious.
   a who   b which   c where

3 The girl ______________ joined our class last week is from Bodrum.
   a who   b which   c where

4 The video game ______________ I bought at the weekend is brilliant.
   a who   b which   c where

5 The town ______________ my grandparents live is high in the mountains.
   a who   b which   c where

6 The boy ______________ lives next door to us plays the harp really well.
   a who   b which   c where

2 **Tick ☑ the correct sentences.**

1 a Yesterday I bought a keyboard which is from the US. ☑
b Yesterday I bought a keyboard who is from the US. ☐
2 a Look, there's the girl where lives next door to my grandparents! ☐
b Look, there's the girl who lives next door to my grandparents! ☐
3 a The car which my brother drives is black. ☐
b The car who my brother drives is black. ☐
4 a Martina is the girl who comes from the north of Spain. ☐
b Martina is the girl where comes from the north of Spain. ☐
5 a The park which we play tennis is near my house. ☐
b The park where we play tennis is near my house. ☐
6 a The instrument who Furkan plays is the piano. ☐
b The instrument which Furkan plays is the piano. ☐

3 **Complete the information about the festival with *who*, *which* or *where*.**

Summer Fest

Summer Fest is for people (1) ___**who**___ love all types of music. It's the festival (2) ______________ everyone enjoys!

We've got jazz, pop, rock, classical and hip-hop. Oh, and folk too! And we've got the perfect location. Hendrix Hall is the place (3) ______________ the festival happens. It's got a lake, tree-lined walks and lots of picnic spots.

Tickets cost £60. For people (4) ______________ are under 16, we've even got a special price: £45!

Mat and Jen are the people (5) ______________ organise the festival. They know everything! If you want to ask them a question, email them at matandjen@summerfestival.com. But the only thing (6) ______________ you really need to know is this: be ready to dance! See you there.

Reading: an advertisement

1 **Read the advertisement, then complete the sentences.**

The perfect guitar for Rock and Roll!

Des Paul designed **The Fretocaster** in 1956.

It's the instrument of the guitar heroes who made musical history.

Today, well-known guitarists such as Peter Brown, Derek Cloptan and Johnny Book play this beautiful instrument.

And now it can be yours for a **very special price!**

For <u>one week only</u> you can buy your very own Des Paul for £350! That's 50% cheaper than normal! What are you waiting for? Buy a Des Paul Fretocaster now!

Available in all good music shops or at
www.despaul.com.

Wow! Whose guitar is that?

It's *mine*!

1 Des Paul created the guitar in ___1956___.
2 Many famous ____________ play the Des Paul.
3 It usually costs ____________.
4 You can buy it for a special price: ____________.
5 The special price is available for only ____________.
6 You can buy the guitar online or in ____________.

Writing

1 **Add more instruments to the instrument word families below.**

String family	guitar,
Percussion family	
Brass family	

Help with Writing

Adverts try to make readers feel something. When we are excited or happy, advertisers think we are more likely to want to spend money. Look at the advert for the guitar. The Des Paul is 'beautiful' and it's 'the instrument of guitar heroes'. The advert uses these phrases to make people want to own one of the guitars.

2 **Write an advertisement for a musical instrument. Use the advertisement for the Fretocaster to help you write yours. Include:**

- The name of the instrument.
- The people who play it.
- The places where you can buy it.
- The types of music which you can play with it.
- The price.

Listening: music

1 15 Listen and tick ☑ the correct picture.

1 Which guitar is Henry's?

2 Which tambourine does Kate play?

3 Which instrument is Lily going to play?

4 Which keyboard is Tony's?

5 Which instrument does Ruby play?

2 16 Listen and match.

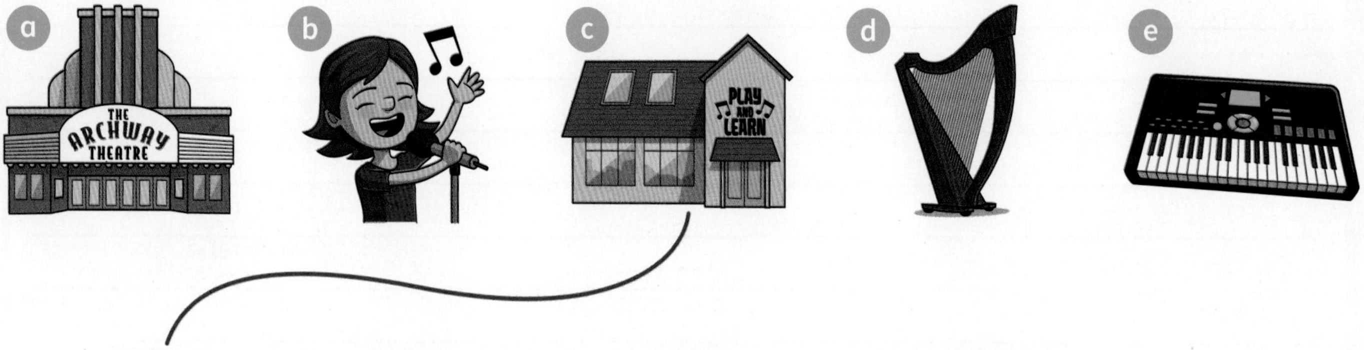

1 Oliver   2 Ava   3 Tim   4 Amelia   5 Lucas

Speaking

1 Look and write. Then play the description game. Use the words in the boxes.

The instrument which I play is small. You hit it or shake it.

You play a percussion instrument – the tambourine!

blow into hit shake pluck

string percussion wind

1 

Harp

2 

____

3 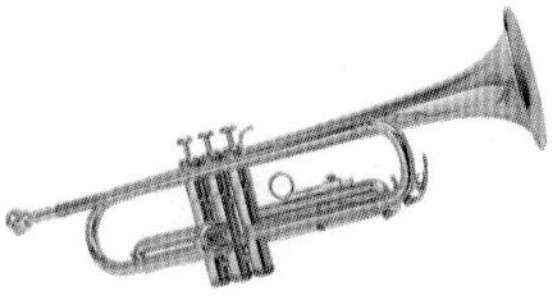

____

4 

____

5 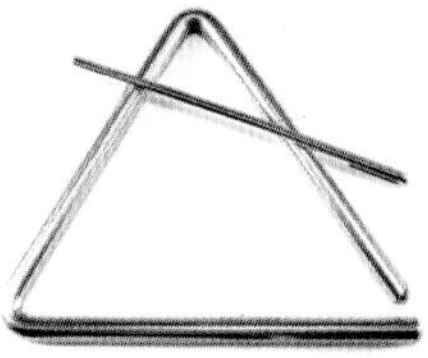

____

6 

____

2 Draw a special musical instrument. Complete and practise.

This is called a ________________.
It's a (string / percussion / wind)
________________ instrument.
It's (big / small) ________________ and it
looks like ________________.
To play it, you have to ________________.

Help with Speaking

When you describe an object, say the object's name. Then you can talk about its size, shape and colour. You can also tell people how it works and how to use it.

3 Talk about your musical instrument.

This is called a key guitar. It's a string and a percussion instrument. It's big and it looks like a box. To play it, you have to pluck the strings and hit the keys.

8 Will

Language focus

Use **will** to make predictions about the future, e.g. *I think Patrick **will** be a football player.*

Yes/No question form:

***Will** we live on the moon one day?*
*Yes, we **will**. / No, we won't.*

'Wh' question form:

***What will** the weather be like next week?* *I think it **will** be hot and sunny.*

The contracted form of **will** is **'ll**, e.g. **I'll**, **she'll**, **we'll**.

Both **will** and **going to** can be used to make predictions. We usually use **going to** when we are more certain that something is going to happen. For example, looking up at a black cloud in the sky, we say, 'It's going to rain', not ~~'It will rain'~~.

1 Complete the sentences with the verbs from the box.

have	travel	be	live	~~catch~~	work

1 Will you **catch** dangerous criminals when you're a police officer, Jess?
2 When I grow up, I'll ________ in a hospital.
3 Will we all ________ on the moon one day?
4 I think it will ________ hot at the weekend.
5 When I grow up, my friends and I will ________ around the world.
6 We'll ________ lots of fun at Elliot's birthday party.

2 **Rewrite the sentences with the words in the correct order.**

1 be / what / you / will — What will you be ?
2 you / will / where / work — ________ ?
3 will / live / another country / in / you — ________ ?
4 you / of house / will / what type / in / live — ________ ?
5 meet / you / who / will — ________ ?
6 where / will / travel / you — ________ ?
7 learn / will / you / what / languages — ________ ?
8 will / you / what / do / your / free time / in — ________ ?

3 **Answer the questions in Activity 2 so they are true for you.**

My future blog

My future

I was thinking about my future the other day. These are my predictions for my life …

1 ________
2 ________
3 ________
4 ________
5 ________
6 ________
7 ________
8 ________

Adverbs

It was the last day of school before the summer holidays. The children walked home, singing songs **loudly** in the afternoon sun.

Language focus

Use **adverbs** to say how someone does, did or will do an action, e.g. *The ambulance driver drove* ***quickly***.

We form many adverbs by adding **-ly** to an adjective:

quick – quick**ly** bad – bad**ly** loud – loud**ly**

If an adjective ends in **y**, we change the **y** to an **i** and add **-ly**:

angry – angr**ily** happy – happ**ily** heavy – heav**ily**

Some adverbs have an irregular form:

good – well hard – hard fast – fast

1 **Write the adverbs.**

1 quick quickly
2 dangerous ________
3 beautiful ________
4 careful ________
5 bad ________
6 heavy ________

2 **Complete the email with the adverb form of the words from the box.**

good ~~quiet~~ loud happy slow quick

To siobhan.odonnell@redworld.com From liam.kerr@zmail.com

Subject Our trip to the planetarium

Hi, Aunt Siobhan

The other night, my friends and I went with our parents to a special 'Evening with the Stars' event at the planetarium in town. We met Neil Collins. He used to be an astronaut! He gave us a tour, but he spoke so (1) quietly that we couldn't hear him very (2) ______________. We wanted to say, 'Please could you speak more (3) ______________, Mr Collins?' but we were all very nervous because he was a famous astronaut.

We saw lots of very interesting things. My favourite was a huge telescope. Mr Collins let us move it around. We looked at one part of the night sky, then another. It was very heavy, so we could only move it really (4) ______________. It needed two of us to move it! We were about to go when Mr Collins called us back. 'Come (5) ______________, everyone. Look, you can see Venus! It's so clear we don't even need the telescope!' We all looked up (6) ______________, so excited to be with this famous astronaut who was telling us all about the planets. When I got home, I downloaded his special space app!

Love, Liam

3 **Complete the sentences with adverbs.**

1 My grandad drove so slowly that it took us a long time to get home.

2 My brother ran ______________ and won the race.

3 I walked ______________ downstairs because I didn't want anyone to hear me.

4 Hold that vase ______________, Tom! You don't want to drop it.

5 My sister did ______________ in her English exam. She got 89%!

6 I played ______________ and lost the tennis match 6–2, 6–1.

Reading: a diary entry

1 **Read Jana's diary and write *t* (true) or *f* (false). Correct the false sentences.**

Wednesday 16th March

'Please come,' said Emre. 'It will be brilliant!'

'But I don't like films about space,' I said.

'Everyone is going. Come on, Jana. We'll have a good time.'

I really didn't want to go the cinema this afternoon. All my friends get so excited about films with special effects, but I find that sort of thing really boring. You know, astronauts on space stations, rockets whizzing through the sky, explosions, UFOs. It's not for me. I said to Emre, 'It will be really boring.'

'Well,' he said slowly, 'maybe it will be boring, but there is only one way to find out.'

The film is called *The Comet*. It's about an astronaut who has to fix her space station,

then ride a comet across space to save Earth from some aliens. Really, really silly. But I loved it! Emre laughed at me after the film because I was talking so much and so quickly. 'And that bit with the two moons, and the scene when the astronaut went up in the rocket through the stars, and, and ...!'

'You see?' said Emre. 'I knew you would have a good time!'

1 Emre didn't want Jana to go to the cinema.

[f] He asked her to go to the cinema.

2 Jana didn't want to go to the cinema.

[ ] ______________________

3 Jana likes films about space.

[ ] ______________________

4 Jana thought the idea for the film was very interesting.

[ ] ______________________

5 Jana liked the film.

[ ] ______________________

1 **Complete the sentences from the diary with the words from the box.**

everyone brilliant be 'll ~~come~~

1 Please come.
2 It will be ______.
3 ______ is going.
4 We ______ have a good time.
5 It will ______ really boring.

Help with Writing

People often write diaries to record not only their feelings but also the most interesting things that they do. This means that in the future, they can look back at the past and remember some of their favourite times.

2 **Write a diary entry for one day last week. Try to use *will* and adverbs. Choose one of the following two events to write about:**

- You went to the cinema with your friends. You watched a film about an astronaut. You wanted to go but didn't like the film.
- You went to the planetarium with your family. You learned about the planets. You didn't want to go, but you had a good time.

Listening: astronauts

1 17 **Listen to the astronaut's story. Complete the sentences.**

1 Robert was on the Moon X27 __mission__.
2 Rachel is the newest ______ on Robert's team.
3 The team's ______ wasn't working and they couldn't fix it.
4 The team couldn't talk to the astronauts on the ______ ______.
5 Robert listened ______ to Rachel's idea.
6 Rachel's idea worked and the team came back home ______.

2 18 **Listen to the interview. Answer the questions.**

1 Why is Rachel famous now?
Because she helped to fix the Moon X27 rocket.
2 What will Rachel and her team do next?
______
3 What does Rachel say about space missions?
______
4 Where will Rachel go on her next mission?
______
5 When will her next mission be?
______
6 Who will go with Rachel on the mission?
______
______
______

1 Read the predictions. Talk about them with a friend.

In the future …

1 people will go on holiday to the moon.
2 we will travel on rockets.
3 there will be a telescope in every home.
4 some people will live on Mars.
5 astronauts will find life on another planet.

Will people go on holiday to the moon? What do you think?

I don't think they will. But I think we'll travel on rockets.

2 With your friend, imagine you are astronauts. What do you need for your space mission? Use the ideas in the box and your ideas.

We need a telescope.

Why?

a telescope	a walkie-talkie	a football
spacesuits	computer games	

It will help us to look at stars and comets. What about a walkie-talkie?

3 With your friend, plan your space mission. Where would you like to go? Decide on three places.

Let's go to the moon first.

Great idea! What about the International Space Station next?

4 Talk about your space mission.

Paula and I will go to the moon first. Next, we'll …

9 a bottle / can / loaf / packet / piece of ...

Language focus

Use **a bottle** / **can** / **loaf** / **packet** / **piece of** to talk about the quantity of something or what something is contained in.

Use **bottle of** with water, orange juice, lemonade, milk.

Use **can of** with lemonade, tomatoes, pears, carrots.

Use **loaf of** with bread. The plural of **loaf** is **loaves**.

Use **packet of** with biscuits, crisps.

Use **piece of** with cheese, cake.

1 Correct the sentences.

1 Can we take a loaf of biscuits, please?

Can we take a packet of biscuits, please?

2 I'm going to buy a bottle of tomatoes from the shop.

____

3 Who would like this last can of cheese?

____

4 We need a bottle of crisps and some chocolate.

____

5 I'd like two cans of bread, please.

____

6 There was a new piece of milk in the fridge yesterday.

____

2 **Complete the dialogue with the words from the box.**

piece	bottles	packets	bottle	~~loaf~~	pieces	packet	loaves

Marie We've got one (1) ___loaf___ of bread. Is that enough?

Carl No, we need two (2) ______________ for the four of us.

Marie OK. What about something to drink?

Carl Well, Stefan's got two (3) ______________ of water and I've got a (4) ______________ of orange juice.

Marie Do we need anything else? A (5) ______________ of biscuits, maybe?

Carl No, Jeremy's got that. You know his sweet tooth. He's going to bring two (6) ______________ of biscuits and a big (7) ______________ of cake for everyone.

Marie Really? I think that's everything, then. Oh, cheese?

Carl Got that. I cut three big (8) ______________ this morning and put them in my bag.

Marie Great!

3 **Use the notes below, and words for containers, to write a shopping list.**

~~2 × bread~~	1 × biscuits	6 × crisps
3 × milk	2 × tomatoes	1 × carrots
2 × water	1 × pears	

Shopping list

1 Two loaves of bread

2 ______________

3 ______________

4 ______________

5 ______________

6 ______________

7 ______________

8 ______________

How much / How many?

Language focus

Use **How much** / **How many?** to ask about the quantity of something, e.g. ***How much*** *cheese do we need?*

Use **how much** with uncountable nouns such as cheese, milk, water, rice.

Use **how many** with countable nouns such as carrots, loaves, packets, pieces.

Note that when we use **how many** with an uncountable noun, we make only the container plural, e.g. *How many bottles of water?* not ~~*How many bottles of waters?*~~

1 **Circle the correct words to complete the sentences.**

1 How *many* / *much* eggs do you need for the omelette?

2 How *many* / *much* bars of chocolate are there in the cupboard?

3 How *many* / *much* pieces of cheese would you like?

4 How *many* / *much* bottles of milk are there in the fridge?

5 How *many* / *much* bread do you want?

6 How *many* / *much* water do you think we need?

2 Match the questions in Activity 1 with the answers below.

a I can see only one. Mum finished the other bottle this morning. [4]

b Get me two small loaves, please. [ ]

c One big piece. [ ]

d I think six will be enough. [ ]

e Quite a lot. It's going to be a hot day. [ ]

f There aren't any. I think Dad ate them all! [ ]

3 Complete the questions about the picture with *much* or *many*. Then answer them with *There is* / *There are*.

1 How __many__ cans of tomatoes are there? __There are two cans of tomatoes.__

2 How ________ packets of crisps are there? ____________________

3 How ________ bread is there? ____________________

4 How ________ chocolate is there? ____________________

5 How ________ apples are there? ____________________

6 How ________ cans of carrots are there? ____________________

Reading: a letter

1 Read the letter, then order the information in sentences a–g.

Dear students,

As you know, next Friday is the camping trip to the Northern Mountains for three days of walking and cooking outdoors. We're all looking forward to it.

I am writing to you in order to give you some important information about the trip. We will set off from the school car park at six o'clock on Friday morning, so please make sure you are at the gates by at least 5.45. That is a very early start, I know – set your alarms!

It will take two hours to drive to the Northern Mountains. Please bring some music to listen to on the journey, a book to read or a game of some type to play with your friends. You should also bring a bottle of water and something to eat, perhaps a sandwich, a piece of fruit and a packet of crisps.

As soon as we get to the campsite, we will put up our tents. The teachers are ready to help students with this. After that, we plan to spend the afternoon outside. There are ropes to swing on and a lake to dive into and swim in. Remember to bring your swimsuits! We are going to organise boat trips throughout the weekend. Students can take turns to sail the small boats.

All students will have special duties over the weekend. Some will make breakfast, others will collect wood. One group will make a big raft. The teachers will tell you on the first day who is in which group.

One final thing. The question students usually ask before the trip is, 'How many people will sleep in each tent?' I can answer that question now. The tents are very big and four students will sleep in each one.

If you would like further information about the trip, do not hesitate to call me in my office between 10 a.m. and 2 p.m., Monday to Friday.

Yours sincerely,

Elanur Berker.

a how long the trip is ☐

b where the students are going ☐

c how many students in a tent ☐

d things students need to bring ☐

e when to call the office ☐

f things students will do in the Northern Mountains ☐

g when the trip starts 1

1 **Answer the questions about your country.**

1 Where are the best places to go camping? ______________________

2 What can you do in those places? ______________________

3 When will the weather be best in those places? ______________________

Help with Writing

When we write formal letters, we begin them with *Dear …*
When a writer wants to be very formal, he or she can finish the letter with *Yours sincerely*.

2 **Imagine you are the principal of a school. You are going to write a letter telling students about a camping trip in your country. Plan the letter by making notes. Include:**

- When it is.
- Where it is.
- How long the trip is.
- Things students need to bring on the trip.
- Activities students will do on the trip.

3 **Now write your letter. Use the letter on the Reading page and your notes from Activity 2 to help you.**

Listening: a camping trip

1 19 **What does Jake want to do at the campsite? Listen and tick ✓ or cross ✗.**

At the campsite, Jake wants to ...

- dive into the lake ☑
- make a fire ☐
- collect wood ☐
- sail a boat ☐
- make a raft ☐
- swing on a rope ☐
- wash and dry clothes ☐
- put up the tent. ☐

2 20 **Listen to Suzie and her dad. Circle the correct answers.**

1 How much water have they got?
 a Four bottles. (b) Five bottles.

2 How much bread have they got?
 a Two loaves. b Three loaves.

3 How many cans of soup are there?
 a Five. b Six.

4 Is there any rice in the box?
 a Yes, there's one packet. b No, there isn't any.

5 What fruit does Suzie want?
 a Bananas. b Apples.

6 How much chocolate do they take?
 a Two small bars. b Two big bars.

Speaking

1 **Imagine you are going on a camping trip. What would you like to take? Draw four things and say.**

I'd like to take my book, a bar of chocolate …

2 **Look and tick ✓ six things you need for your camping trip. Then ask a friend and tick ✓ the things they need.**

Do you need any pasta?

Yes, I do. What about you?

I don't. But I need some bread.

Food and drink	Me	My friend
pasta		
bread		
water		
milk		
apples		
soup		
tomatoes		
eggs		

3 **With your friend, look at your table in Activity 2. Ask and answer questions with *How much* and *How many*.**

How much pasta do you need?

I need two packets. How much bread do you need?

I need four loaves.

Audioscripts

Welcome Unit page 10

01

Daisy Mike, do you like going on adventures?

Mike Yes, of course, Daisy! Adventures are exciting!

Daisy So, what do you like doing?

Mike Well, I like walking in the mountains. I always discover amazing places and animals in the mountains.

Daisy Wow! Who do you go with?

Mike I go with my cousins, every summer. They live near the mountains. You can come next summer!

Daisy Hmm, thanks, but I don't really like the mountains … I prefer the city – I like riding the big roller coaster at the funfair!

Mike The big roller coaster? Really? I hate going on that one. I'm scared of it! But I love driving the dodgem cars. What about you?

Daisy Me too! The dodgem cars are fun!

Mike And I also like looking for treasure. My brother and I are good at finding treasure in different places.

Daisy Hmm … I don't like doing that. I never find any treasure! But I like exploring caves. What about you, Mike?

Mike Of course! I love exploring caves. Last weekend, I found some bats in one!

Daisy What an adventure! Let's plan an exploring trip!

Mike Yes! What about next weekend?

Daisy Great idea!

02

Jess Hi, Jacob. How was your climbing trip?

Jacob It was amazing, Jess!

Jess Did you go to Castle Mountain?

Jacob No, we didn't. We went to Cave Mountain.

Jess Wow! Cave Mountain is far. How did you get there? Did you go by train?

Jacob No, we didn't. My mum drove. I saw lots of beautiful trees and flowers from the car and I took lots of photos.

Jess That's nice! Were you with your brother?

Jacob No, my brother didn't come. He had a football match. I went there with my mum and dad.

Jess Was the climb fun?

Jacob Yes, it was fun! But it was dangerous, too – it started to rain when we were at the top. We were wet! I was scared, but my dad helped me to walk down.

Jess Oh dear! So, how long did you walk for?

Jacob We walked for four hours! Two hours to go up and two hours to go down. I was tired at the end!

Jess Sure, that's a long walk!

Jacob Yes! Now my parents want to climb Treasure Mountain.

Jess Treasure Mountain is fantastic!

Jacob Yes, I know. But I'd like to climb Diamond Mountain.

Jess Wow! I don't know Diamond Mountain, but I'd like to climb it with you!

Jacob Of course!

Unit 1 page 18

03

Security guard Hello! And welcome to the Shield Museum.

Girl Thank you!

Security guard OK. Before you go in, I must tell you the rules at the museum.

Girl OK.

Security guard Right. First, you must show your ticket to the woman at the door. Have you got your ticket?

Girl Yes, I have. Look.

Security guard Good! Now, there are a lot of very old shields in the museum. Some are more than six hundred years old.

Girl Wow! That's amazing!

Security guard You can look at the shields, but you mustn't touch them. OK?

Girl OK. No touching, then. But can I take photos of the shields?

Security guard Oh, I'm sorry but you can't. You mustn't take photos of the shields. But there are lots of postcards in the shop – you can buy the ones that show your favourite shields. Ah! And I see that you're carrying a bag.

Girl Yes. Can I take my bag into the museum?

Security guard No, I'm sorry … You must leave your bag in a locker. You mustn't carry bags inside the museum.

Girl Fine. I'd like to see some very famous shields. Are there any?

Security guard Yes, of course! There are a lot of very interesting shields. Some famous kings used them in their fights!

Girl Great! Oh! One more question: what time does the museum close?

Security guard The museum closes at five o'clock. You've got lots of time. Enjoy your visit!

Girl Thanks!

04

Hi! I'm Kasim. Guess what? Our class went to the Knight Museum yesterday. The museum was fantastic, but we had some problems at the beginning. First, we went to see the helmets. There were some amazing helmets on a shelf. I was with my friend William. William took one of the helmets and put it on! When the woman from the museum saw William, she came and told him, 'Take that helmet off, please. You mustn't touch the helmets, shields or swords in this museum.' When our teacher, Mr Martin, saw the woman, he ran to talk to her. But the woman told him, 'You mustn't run in this museum!' She wasn't happy! Well! The rest of our visit was fine – we didn't touch things, didn't run and didn't shout. Then, on the bus back to school, William said, 'Sorry, Mr Martin. I only wanted to be a knight.' So Mr Martin told William, 'You can be a knight in the school play.' But William wasn't happy – he loves knights, but he doesn't like acting!

Unit 2 page 26

05

Hi! You know, I had a really nice weekend in the countryside. My parents and I went to a forest near our house. We walked on a long path through the forest. There were some beautiful trees and autumn leaves! We walked near a village, but we didn't stop there. When we came out of the forest, we saw a big mountain in front of us. We wanted to see the view from the top, so we climbed up the mountain. The view was amazing! We could see everything: the fields, the forest and the village. I took lots of photos! We walked down the mountain and we were hungry, so we looked for a place to eat. We found a nice field and had our picnic there. When we finished our picnic, it started to rain! We ran to the village because the rain was heavy. In the village, we found a lovely café and we had some cake there. It was a great way to end our adventure!

06

Leo Milly, look at this photo of me playing football.

Milly Oh! You're a really good football player, Leo! How old were you in the photo?

Leo I was six. Now I can play tennis, too. But I couldn't play tennis when I was six.

Milly I see. What other sports could you do when you were six?

Leo Well, I could swim. I learned when I was five – with you!

Milly That's right! I enjoyed our swimming lessons. They were fun! Hey, could you play the guitar then?

Leo No, I couldn't. I started guitar lessons when I was seven. And I couldn't ride a bike! I only learned last summer! But I could ride a scooter. I loved riding my scooter!

Milly Yes, I remember! And I was very good at skipping, but you couldn't skip.

Leo True! I couldn't skip when I was six, and I can't skip now. It's difficult!

Milly Haha! But you could fly a kite when you were six. And that's not easy!

Leo That's right. When I was six, I was really good at flying kites. My dad taught me!

Unit 3 page 34

07

Hi! I'm going to tell you about last Sunday – my friends and I were in danger! It all happened in the park near home. I went there with my friends, Leah and John. The trees in that park are really tall, and the tallest tree is next to a river. We climbed that tree and … we got to the top! It was raining, but we were having fun. Suddenly, the rain turned into a heavy storm. We looked down at the river – there was a flood! There was water everywhere! And there was a very strong wind! We were trying to climb down, but it was very difficult. We weren't feeling happy any more. Luckily, Leah had her phone and she called her parents. But she also called the emergency services. Some time later, our parents came, and a fire engine arrived too. A firefighter put a tall ladder up against the tree. She climbed up and helped us to come down from the tree. It was exciting, but we were scared, too. The firefighter told us, 'Next time, check the weather before you climb a tree!'

08

1 **Mary** What were you doing yesterday at 3 o'clock, Theo?

Theo I was watching a film called *Fire!* It was fantastic. What about you, Mary?

Mary I was reading a book.

2 **Boy** Amy, did you see the TV programme about floods? It was at 4 o'clock.

Amy No, I didn't. I was playing football!

Boy You should watch it online. It was really interesting.

3 **Miss Parker** You didn't come to school yesterday, Jamie. Why?

Jamie I wasn't feeling well, Miss Parker.

Miss Parker Oh, I'm sorry to hear that. Are you OK now?

Jamie Yes, I am! Thanks!

4 **Harry** Eva, what were you doing yesterday afternoon? Were you playing on your new games console?

Eva No, I wasn't, Harry! I was doing the homework about the emergency services. Remember?

Harry Oh, no! I forgot to do the homework!

5 **Girl** Freddie, what time were you having breakfast yesterday?

Freddie At 12 o'clock.

Girl At 12 o'clock? That's late! What were you doing before?

Freddie I was sleeping!

6 **Grandpa** How was the beach this morning, Rosie?

Rosie Oh, it wasn't great, Grandpa.

Grandpa Really? Why?

Rosie Because it was raining. We went to a village near the beach. And it wasn't raining there!

Unit 4 page 42

09

Woman Good morning. How can I help you?

Samuel Hello. Can I have two single tickets to Cambridge, please?

Woman Yes, of course. Did you say two single tickets?

Samuel Yes, that's right. One ticket is for me and the other one is for my mum. She's buying a cup of coffee at the moment. She loves coffee!

Woman Ah, I see!

Samuel How much is that?

Woman That's £9, please.

Samuel £9. OK. Here you go.

Woman Thank you. Here are your tickets. You need to go to Platform number 2.

Samuel Thanks. Where's Platform 2?

Woman Go up the escalator and over the bridge. The platform is right there.

Samuel Great. Oh! What time does the next train leave?

Woman Hmm … let me see. The next train to Cambridge is … at 10. That's right, at 10 o'clock. You've got a big rucksack and a suitcase there. Do you need help?

Samuel I'm OK, thanks! My mum is coming back from the café now.

10

Every year, my dad and I go to the theatre in London. That's one of the best days of the year. Last Saturday was 'theatre day' for me and Dad. At nine in the morning, we were at the station. We were very excited! We got our tickets to go to London. Then Dad bought a cup of tea and he bought me an apple juice. Our train arrived at Platform 1, but Dad was worried. He was looking for our theatre tickets and he couldn't find them. We got on the train and found our seats. When the train left the station, Dad was looking really worried. 'I haven't got our tickets!' he said. We got to London and walked to the theatre, but we were feeling sad – we didn't have tickets for the play! 'Let's buy new tickets,' Dad said. At the theatre, lots of people were waiting in front of the ticket office. When it was our turn, Dad said to the man at the desk, 'I had two tickets for today, but I think I lost them.' 'What's your name, sir?' said the man. 'Jonathan Gray,' said Dad. Then the man said, 'I've got your tickets here, Mr Gray. You asked to pick them up at the theatre. Here you are.' That was a great surprise! Right then, Dad and I walked up the stairs to our seats. And we really enjoyed the play!

Unit 5 page 50

11

Boy So, what happened yesterday, Kelly?

Kelly Well, my mum and I were looking for a birthday present for my dad. We wanted to buy him a special pen and some nice notebooks. My dad's a journalist. He writes his stories on the computer now, but he used to have lots of notebooks and he used to collect different pens.

Boy Sounds nice! So, which shop did you go to?

Kelly Oh, we were in a pen shop. It's new and it's called Write Now. It used to be a clothes shop. It's next to the sports centre.

Boy Oh! I think I know it.

Kelly Well, when my mum and I were choosing a notebook, we saw a woman. She looked strange. She was putting some pens in her bag! And they were really expensive ones!

Boy Oh dear!

Kelly Yes! She was tall with long blonde hair and she had a scar on her cheek.

Boy Wow! So what did you do?

Kelly My mum told the shop assistant. But at that moment, the woman wasn't in the shop anymore. The shop assistant phoned the police. They came very quickly and asked us some questions.

Boy Did they catch the woman?

Kelly No, they didn't. But I hope that they do!

Boy Your dad has to write a story about that!

12

Teacher OK, Max, it's your turn. Tell us, what would you like to do when you're older?

Max I'd like to be a police officer when I grow up. My Aunt Vicky is a photographer now, but she used to be a police officer, and I want to be just like her. Auntie Vicky was a police officer for ten years. She was in danger many times, so she had to be careful. And she used to work all night! But my aunt liked doing her job and helping people. She had to wear a special navy blue uniform and she had a cool walkie-talkie. I remember she used to carry it everywhere! My aunt also used to drive a police car to chase criminals. And she caught more than one! Look – this is a photo of Auntie Vicky as a police officer. She looked very different! Her hair used to be dark and straight, you see? It's blonde and curly now!

Teacher That's great, Max. I didn't know the story about your aunt. She can teach you to be the best police officer in town!

Unit 6 page 58

13

OK, children. Let's start the story. Once upon a time, there was a terrible beast. It lived in a cave, in a faraway forest. The beast had a long black tail, and its tongue was yellow. The people from the village near the forest were very scared of that creature. They called it 'the Terrible Omnix' and said to visitors, 'You must not go into the forest.' The Terrible Omnix had big wings. Its neck was thick and long. And there were scales, lots of scales, on the beast's back. And on its head, there were three short horns. Some people said that the Omnix looked like a dragon. They said that it was the biggest dragon in the forest. One day, a girl from the village went into the forest. Her name was Maya. Would you like to listen to her story? Well …

14

Laura Edward, can I see your book?

Edward Yes, here you are, Laura.

Laura *The Terrible Omnix*. It looks interesting.

Edward It's great! It's about a girl called Maya. She goes into a forest and finds strange beasts and creatures there.

Laura Why is the book called *The Terrible Omnix*?

Edward Well, the Omnix is the biggest and most dangerous beast in the forest. He looks like a dragon. But there are other creatures, too. First, Maya finds a small beast and she calls it the Munkle. Then she meets two creatures that look like crocodiles, and she calls them the Trussock and the Arkle. The Trussock and the Arkle are bigger than the Munkle. The Munkle is the smallest beast in the forest, and it looks like a monkey.

Laura Wow! Can I look at these beasts? I like their names – they're funny!

Edward Yes, sure! Look, here they are. They're really cool, but my favourite beast is called the Galloping Runnyback.

Laura The Galloping Runnyback? What does that one look like? Can I see?

Edward Sure! Here it is. It looks like a horse, you see? I think its wings are fantastic! The Galloping Runnyback is the most beautiful creature in the forest. It's more beautiful than the Ginocat. And it's faster, too. But the fastest beast is the Gagger. The Gagger looks like a dinosaur!

Laura Like which dinosaur? Like a stegosaurus?

Edward No. The Gagger looks like a T-Rex.

Laura Wow! It's a great book, Edward. Can I read it when you finish it?

Edward Of course!

Unit 7 page 66

15

1 **Girl** Is the purple guitar yours, Henry?

Henry No, it isn't. That's Jake's. And Sam's is the orange one.

Girl Is the black guitar yours, then?

Henry Yes, my guitar is the black one.

2 **Boy** Is this yellow tambourine yours, Kate?

Kate No, it isn't. It's Tom's.

Boy Are you sure it's his?

Kate Yes, I am. Tom plays his yellow tambourine every day.

Boy OK. So is the brown tambourine yours?

Kate No, mine is the white tambourine. I don't like brown!

3 **Man** Lily, would you like to play the trumpet?

Lily Hmm … I'm not sure about the trumpet. Can I play the violin?

Man Hmm … I need someone for the drums. Do you like the drums?

Lily Yes, I do! OK, I can play the drums.

Man Great! Thanks, Lily.

4 **Girl** OK, here is my red keyboard. Now, is the green keyboard yours, Tony?

Tony No, it isn't mine. The green keyboard is Carmen's.

Girl OK. So this blue keyboard is …

Tony Mine!

Girl Oh! I like your blue keyboard, Tony!

5 **Ronnie** Do you play a musical instrument, Ruby?

Ruby Yes, I do. Guess!

Ronnie Hmm … You play the guitar!

Ruby No! I play the piano. What about you, Ronnie?

Ronnie I play the recorder. But I think the piano is more exciting!

16

1 **Girl** Look! That's the school where Oliver goes.
Boy Really?
Girl Yes. It's a special music school. They learn to play different musical instruments.
Boy That's great!

2 **Girl** Is this the theatre where Ivy played in the orchestra?
Boy Yes, that's right. It's called the Archway Theatre.

3 **Girl** Where are you going, Tim?
Tim I'm going to see Ava.
Girl Who's Ava?
Tim Ava is the girl who sang at the party last night. Do you remember?
Girl Oh, yes! She's a great singer!

4 **Boy** OK, Amelia. Look – all these instruments are ours.
Amelia Ours?
Boy Well, they are the school's, but we can play them.
Amelia Any of them? I'd like to play the harp!

5 **Girl** Is that instrument yours, Lucas?
Lucas No, it isn't. That's my sister's. But look, the instrument which I play is over there. On the desk.
Girl Wow! Do you play the keyboard?
Lucas Yes, I do! Do you want to try it?

Unit 8 page 74

17

I'm Robert, one of the astronauts on the Moon X27 mission. We are back on our planet safely now, and it was all thanks to Rachel. Rachel is the newest astronaut on my team. And Moon X27 was her first mission. So, two weeks ago we were on the moon. Our rocket wasn't working and we didn't know how to fix it. And our communications system was working really badly, so we couldn't talk to the astronauts on the space station. We needed help. And we needed it quickly! Then Rachel had an idea. She started to press some buttons and make some notes. After some time, Rachel said, 'I think the rocket will work again.' I listened carefully. Rachel said, 'First, you press this. Then you move that very slowly. After that, you test this part of the rocket. Finally, you turn this on. Now, the screen should go blue …' And the screen went blue! The rocket was working again and we could go home happily!

18

Interviewer Hello, and welcome back to Earth, Rachel!
Rachel Thank you.
Interviewer You're a very famous astronaut now. You helped to fix the Moon X27 rocket!
Rachel Well, thanks! I had the idea, but we all worked hard together to come back home!
Interviewer That's amazing. So, what will you and your team do next?
Rachel Well, I think we'll look carefully at the Moon X27 rocket. We want to know why the rocket stopped working. All space missions have to be safe for astronauts.
Interviewer Sure. And will you go to the moon again?
Rachel Yes, I will. But I think my next mission will be on Mars.
Interviewer Will you travel to Mars?
Rachel Yes, I think that will be next year. The mission is called Mars X14. I'll go with some astronauts from the Moon X27 mission.
Interviewer That sounds exciting! Good luck, and thank you for talking to us, Rachel.

Unit 9 page 82

19

Jake We're going to the campsite tomorrow, Mum!
Mum I know! We'll have a great time, Jake.
Jake I want to dive into the lake and swim to the other side.
Mum Great! I'll dive into the lake with you.
Jake Nice! And can we make a fire?
Mum Yes, we can collect wood and make a fire.
Jake That will be cool! Can we sail a boat, too?
Mum Well, we can sail a boat, or we can make a raft.
Jake Wow! OK, I don't want to sail a boat. I want to make a raft!
Mum OK. Let's make a raft! Look, Jake – it says here that you can swing on a rope at the campsite. Would you like to do that?
Jake Hmm … No, thanks Mum. I don't like swinging on ropes.
Mum OK. Hmm …
Jake What are you thinking, Mum?
Mum You can wash and dry your clothes at the campsite.
Jake Oh, Mum! No! I don't want to wash or dry clothes!
Mum Haha! No problem, Jake. You don't have to do that. But you can help to put up the tent.
Jake That's exciting, Mum! I'll put up the tent with you and Dad.

20

Dad Right, Suzie. Let's pack the food and drink for our camping trip.
Suzie OK, Dad!
Dad How many bottles of water have we got? Can you look in the fridge?
Suzie OK. We've got … two, three, four … five. Five bottles of water.
Dad Great! Now, the bread is in that box. Are there two loaves?
Suzie Let me see … We've got three loaves of bread, Dad. And there are some cans of soup. Let me count them. One, two … five, six – there are six cans of soup.
Dad That's good. Is there any rice in the box?
Suzie Oh, yes, Dad. Here it is. We've got one packet of rice.
Dad OK, that's great.
Suzie Dad, can we take some bananas?
Dad Of course! Let's take some bananas. And we can buy some apples at the campsite.
Suzie OK. And what about some chocolate?
Dad Good idea. Let's take two small bars of chocolate – one bar for you and the other one for me, OK? There aren't any big bars.
Suzie Mmm! That's nice, Dad!

Acknowledgements

The authors and publishers acknowledge the following sources of copyright material and are grateful for the permissions granted. While every effort has been made, it has not always been possible to identify the sources of all the material used, or to trace all copyright holders. If any omissions are brought to our notice, we will be happy to include the appropriate acknowledgements on reprinting and in the next update to the digital edition, as applicable.

Key: ST = Starter, U = Unit

Photography

The following images are sourced from Getty Images.

ST: Tetra Images; Juanmonino/iStock/Getty Images Plus; Robert Niedring/Alloy; ViewStock; Artur Debat/Moment; Robert Niedring/MITO images; Rainer Dittrich; Sebastian Condrea/Moment; Westend61; **U1:** skodonnell/E+; Ng Sok Lian/EyeEm; bob_sato_1973/iStock/Getty Images Plus; MikeyGen73/iStock/Getty Images Plus; Sean Gladwell/Moment; dja65/iStock/Getty Images Plus; Donald Iain Smith/Blend Images; charlybutcher/iStock/Getty Images Plus; RMAX/iStock/Getty Images Plus; Westend61; Lorenzo Dominguez/Moment; Lee Harris/EyeEm; **U2:** Imgorthand/E+; Mint Images/Mint Images RF; Stephen Dorey/The Image Bank; GCShutter/E+; kali9/E+; Erika Fournier/EyeEm; Martin Ruegner/The Image Bank; **U3:** PaulJRobinson/iStock/Getty Images Plus; Marizza/iStock/Getty Images Plus; Merethe Svarstad Eeg/EyeEm; hsvrs/iStock/Getty Images Plus; Thinkstock/Stockbyte; ChrisCrafter/E+; **U4:** Madhourse/iStock/Getty Images Plus; Bim/iStock/Getty Images Plus; Chris Mellor/Lonely Planet Images/Getty Images Plus; MonicaNinker/iStock/Getty Images Plus; **U5:** aijohn784/iStock/Getty Images Plus; lillisphotography/E+; Oppenheim Bernhard/Stone/Getty Images Plus; **U6**: Alphotographic/iStock/Getty Images Plus; Danita Delimont/Gallo Images/Getty Images Plus; **U7:** C Squared Studios/Photodisc; Francesco Milanese/iStock/Getty Images Plus; Trodler/iStock/Getty Images Plus; bevrnja/iStock/Getty Images Plus; Hogie/iStock/Getty Images Plus; mrdoggs/iStock/Getty Images Plus; **U8:** Maike Hildebrandt/iStock/Getty Images Plus; KrisCole/iStock/Getty Images Plus; 1971yes/iStock/Getty Images Plus; Nick White/DigitalVision; **U9:** miljko/E+; Jamie Grill/Photodisc; Anton Petrus/Moment.

The following image is sourced from another library.

U1: Andrey Kuzmin/Alamy Stock Photo.

Illustrations

A Corazon Abierto (Sylvie Poggio Artists); Clive Goodyer (Beehive Illustration); Anna Hancock (Beehive Illustration); Marek Jagucki; Chris Lensch; Alex Patrick (Bright Group); Alan Rowe (Beehive Illustration); David Sem; Dave Smith (Beehive Illustration).

Audio

Audio production by Hart McLeod.

Typeset

EMC Design Limited.

Cover design by We Are Bold.